Cash Crop to Cash Cow

THE HISTORY OF TOBACCO AND SMOKING IN AMERICA

Tobacco: The Deadly Drug

Born to Smoke: Nicotine and Genetics

Burning Money: The Cost of Smoking

But All My Friends Smoke: Cigarettes and Peer Pressure

But Smoking Makes Me Happy: The Link Between Nicotine and Depression

Cash Crop to Cash Cow: The History of Tobacco and Smoking in America

False Images, Deadly Promises: Smoking and the Media

No More Butts: Kicking the Tobacco Habit

Putting Out the Fire: Smoking and the Law

Smokeless Tobacco: Not a Safe Alternative

Teenagers and Tobacco: Nicotine and the Adolescent Brain

Thousands of Deadly Chemicals: Smoking and Health

Cash Crop to Cash Cow

The History of Tobacco and Smoking in America

by
Mary Meinking

Cash Crop to Cash Cow:
The History of Tobacco and Smoking in America

MASON CREST PUBLISHERS INC.
370 Reed Road
Broomall, Pennsylvania 19008
(866)MCP-BOOK (toll free)
www.masoncrest.com

First Printing

9 8 7 6 5 4 3 2 1

ISBN 978-1-4222-0231-9
ISBN 978-1-4222-0230-2 (series)

Library of Congress Cataloging-in-Publication Data

Meinking, Mary.
Cash crop to cash cow : the history of tobacco and smoking in America / Mary Meinking.
p. cm. — (Tobacco : the deadly drug)
Includes bibliographical references and index.
ISBN 978-1-4222-0231-9 ISBN 978-1-4222-1328-5
1. Tobacco—History. 2. Tobacco—Social aspects. 3. Smoking—History. I. Title.
GT3020.M35 2008
362.29'6—dc22

2008013193

Design by MK Bassett-Harvey.
Produced by Harding House Publishing Service, Inc.
www.hardinghousepages.com
Cover design by Peter Culotta.
Printed in The United States of America.

Contents

Introduction

Tobacco has been around for centuries. In fact, it played a major role in the early history of the United States. Tobacco use has fallen into and out of popularity, sometimes based on gender roles or class, or more recently, because of its effects on health. The books in the Mason Crest series TOBACCO: THE DEADLY DRUG, provide readers with a look at many aspects of tobacco use. Most important, the series takes a serious look at why smoking is such a hard habit to break, even with all of the available information about its harmful effects.

The primary ingredient in tobacco products that keeps people coming back for another cigarette is nicotine. Nicotine is a naturally occurring chemical in the tobacco plant. As plants evolved over millions of years, they developed the ability to produce chemical defenses against being eaten by animals. Nicotine is the tobacco plant's chemical defense weapon. Just as too much nicotine can make a person feel dizzy and nauseated, so the same thing happens to animals that might otherwise eat unlimited quantities of the tobacco plant.

Nicotine, in small doses, produces mildly pleasurable (rewarding) experiences, leading many people to dose themselves repeatedly throughout the day. People carefully dose themselves with nicotine to maximize the rewarding experience. These periodic hits of tobacco also help people avoid unpleasant (toxic) effects, such as dizziness, nausea, trembling, and sweating, which can occur when someone takes in an excessive amount of nicotine. These unpleasant effects are sometimes seen when a person smokes for the first time.

Although nicotine is the rewarding component of cigarettes, it is not the cause of many diseases that trouble smokers, such as lung cancer, heart attacks, and strokes. Many of the thousands of other chemicals in the cigarette are responsible for the increased risk for these diseases among smokers. In some cases, medical research has identified cancer-causing chemicals in the burning cigarette. More research is needed, because our understanding of exactly how cigarette smoking causes many forms of cancer, lung diseases (emphysema, bronchitis), heart attacks, and strokes is limited, as is our knowledge on the effects of secondhand smoke.

The problem with smoking also involves addiction. But what is addiction? Addiction refers to a pattern of behavior, lasting months to years, in which a person engages in the intense, daily use of a pleasure-producing (rewarding) activity, such as smoking. This type of use has medically and personally negative effects for the person. As an example of negative medical consequences, consider that heavy smoking (nicotine addiction) leads to heart attacks and lung cancer. As an example of negative personal consequences, consider that heavy smoking may cause a loss of friendship, because the friend can't tolerate the smoke and/or the odor.

Nicotine addiction includes tolerance and withdrawal. New smokers typically start with fewer than five cigarettes per day. Gradually, as the body becomes adapted to the presence of nicotine, greater amounts are required to obtain the same rewarding effects, and the person eventually smokes fifteen to twenty or more cigarettes per day. This is tolerance, meaning that more drug is needed to achieve the same rewarding effects. The brain becomes "wired" differently after long-term exposure to nicotine, allowing the brain to tolerate levels of nicotine that would otherwise be toxic and cause nausea, vomiting, dizziness and anxiety.

When a heavy smoker abruptly stops smoking, irritability, headache, sleeplessness, anxiety, and difficulty concentrating all develop within half a day and trouble the smoker for one to two weeks. These withdrawal effects are generally the opposite of those produced by the drug. They are another external sign that the brain has become wired differently because of long-term exposure to nicotine. The withdrawal effects described above are accompanied by craving. For the nicotine addict, craving is a state of mind in which having a cigarette seems the most important thing in life at the moment. For the nicotine addict, craving is a powerful urge to smoke.

Nicotine addiction, then, can be understood as heavy, daily use over months to years (with tolerance and withdrawal), despite negative consequences. Now that we have definitions of *nicotine* and *addiction*, why read the books in this series? The answer is simple: tobacco is available everywhere to persons of all ages. The books in the series TOBACCO: THE DEADLY DRUG are about understanding the beginnings, natural history, and consequences of nicotine addiction. If a teenager smokes at least one cigarette daily for a month, that person has an 80 percent chance of becoming a lifetime, nicotine-addicted, daily smoker, with all the negative consequences.

But the series is not limited to those topics. What are the characteristic beginnings of nicotine addiction? Nicotine addiction typically begins between the ages of twelve and twenty, when most young people decide to try a first cigarette. Because cigarettes are available everywhere in our society, with little restriction on purchase, nearly everyone is faced with the decision to take a puff from that first cigarette. Whether this first puff leads to a lifetime of nicotine addiction depends on several factors. Perhaps the most important factor is DNA (genetics), as twin studies tell us that most of the risk for nicotine addiction is genetic, but there is a large role for nongenetic factors (environment), such as the smoking habits of friends. Research is needed to identify the specific genetic and environmental factors that shape a person's decision to continue to smoke after that first cigarette. Books in the series also address how peer pressure and biology affect one's likelihood of smoking and possibly becoming addicted.

It is difficult to underestimate the power of nicotine addiction. It causes smokers to continue to smoke despite life-threatening events. When heavy smokers have a heart attack, a life-threatening event often directly related to smoking, they spend a week or more in the hospital where they cannot smoke. So they are discharged after enforced abstinence. Even though they realize that smoking contributed strongly to the heart attack, half of them return to their former smoking habits within three weeks of leaving the hospital. This decision to return to smoking increases the risk of a second heart attack. Nicotine addiction can influence powerfully the choices we make, often prompting us to make choices that put us at risk.

TOBACCO: THE DEADLY DRUG doesn't stop with the whys and the hows of smoking and addiction. The series includes books that provide readers with tools they can use to not take that first cigarette, how they can stand up to negative peer pressure, and know when they are being unfairly influenced by the media. And if they do become smokers, books in the series provide information about how they can stop.

If nicotine addiction can be a powerful negative effect, then giving people information that might help them decide to avoid—or stop—smoking makes sense. That is what TOBACCO: THE DEADLY DRUG is all about.

— *Wade Berrettini MD, PhD*

CHAPTER 1

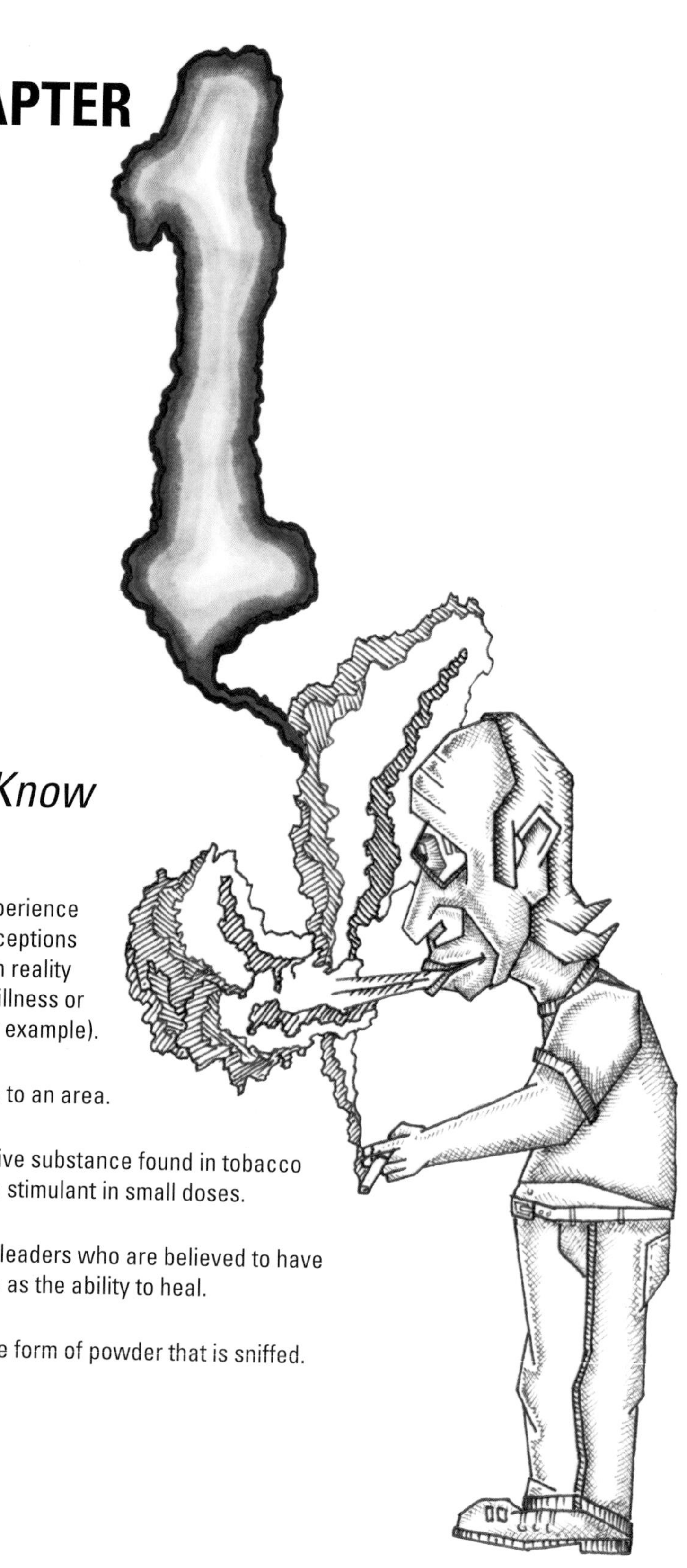

Words to Know

hallucinate: To experience visions or other perceptions that have no basis in reality (because of mental illness or the use of drugs, for example).

indigenous: Native to an area.

nicotine: An addictive substance found in tobacco leaves that acts as a stimulant in small doses.

shamans: Spiritual leaders who are believed to have special powers such as the ability to heal.

snuff: Tobacco in the form of powder that is sniffed.

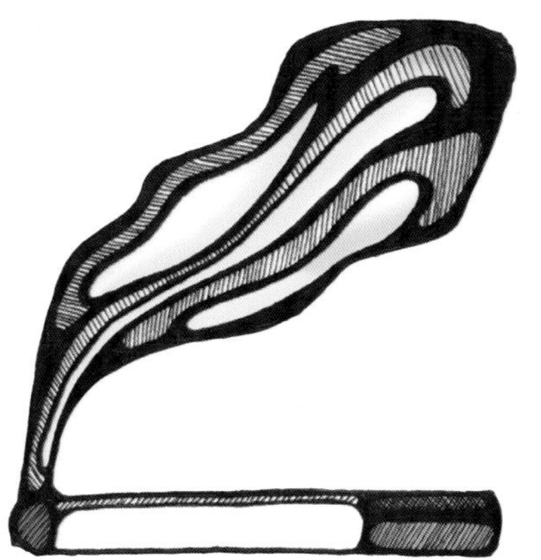

Tobacco Is Born

Without tobacco, America would not be what it is today. This tall, leafy green plant played an important ceremonial role among Native American tribes. Among early European settlers, tobacco acquired great commercial significance—even saving the Jamestown colony from economic ruin in the first decades of the seventeenth century. More than 150 years later, during the Revolutionary War, soldiers in the Continental Army sometimes received their pay in tobacco. And after the United States won independence from Britain, tobacco's importance in American society only increased. By the late nineteenth century the burgeoning popularity of cigarettes—

The tobacco plant has been cultivated for thousands of years; it was originally used as an incense and burned over a fire.

and the invention of a machine for producing them quickly—helped the tobacco industry reap enormous profits. During the twentieth century the number of smokers rose still further, ensuring continued profits for tobacco companies and, because of taxes on cigarettes, putting money into the U.S. Treasury as well as the coffers of state governments. The indisputable link between tobacco use and deadly diseases helped lead to a drop in U.S. smoking rates in the decade 1990–2000. Still, today about one in five American adults is a smoker. Despite setbacks for the industry, tobacco remains a cash cow, a commodity that generates consistent profits.

Sacred Plant

Dozens of species of tobacco are native to the Americas. Scientists aren't certain when *indigenous* peoples in North and South America first began drying and burning the leaves of tobacco plants they found growing in the wild. Estimates of eight thousand or ten thousand years ago have been offered, but some scientists believe tobacco may have been used even earlier.

Tobacco may initially have been burned like incense, with dried tobacco leaves thrown into a fire along with other herbs. The resulting smoke was probably regarded as a sacrificial offering to the spirits. Eventually, however, indigenous people began deliberately taking tobacco smoke into their lungs, either by blowing on the embers of a fire and inhaling, or by smoking dried tobacco in pipes or cigars.

A milestone in the history of tobacco use took place around 6000 BCE to 3000 BCE in the Andes Mountains of Peru, Ecuador, and perhaps eastern Bolivia. There, people first began deliberately cultivating two species of tobacco—*Nicotiana tabacum* and *Nicotiana rustica*—rather than simply gathering plants that grew in the wild.

It might seem surprising that people would devote effort and resources to growing tobacco rather than food crops at a time when farming was very labor intensive. But tobacco was considered a sacred plant. *Shamans*—priests or medicine men who employed magic to cure illnesses, influence events, and communicate with the spirit world—used tobacco in their ceremonies. The connection between tobacco and the supernatural can be explained by the properties of *nicotine*. A chemical compound found naturally in tobacco, nicotine acts as a mild stimulant in small doses. In large doses, however, it can cause people to *hallucinate*.

Seeking to experience visions from the supernatural realm—or even personally to enter the spirit world—shamans consumed large doses of nicotine. Ancient tobacco contained a large amount of nicotine (about 18 percent, compared with 1.5 percent in the tobacco used in cigarettes today). Furthermore, shamans might smoke many cigars in succession. Among some South American tribes, these cigars were up to four feet long. They consisted of tobacco leaves wrapped around and around a stick or banana-leaf stem. They were so heavy that men needed Y-shaped "cigar supports" to hold them up.

But there were other, less strenuous methods for absorbing nicotine into the body. These included placing wet tobacco leaves on the skin; sniffing powdered tobacco, or *snuff*; drinking tea brewed from

Tobacco Cure-All

Native Americans believed tobacco could aid in healing or curing asthma, bad breath, bruises, colic, constipation, convulsions, coughs, cuts, diarrhea, fatigue, fever, gout, headaches, hunger, kidney stones, malaria, miscarriages, pain, paralysis, seizures, sleeplessness, sore muscles, snakebites, sore throat, scorpion stings, stomachaches, toothaches, and even warts.

Shamans would use tobacco in their medicinal ceremonies; they would consume large amounts of nicotine in an attempt to enter the spirit world.

tobacco leaves; and licking a concentrated gel made from tobacco plants.

Shamans' use of tobacco could be quite dangerous. Absorbing too much nicotine can lead to potentially fatal nicotine poisoning.

A Plant of Many Uses

From the Andes region where it first began, the practice of cultivating tobacco gradually spread through trade contacts and migration. And, in part because cultivation made possible a reliable supply of tobacco, uses for the "holy herb" expanded beyond helping shamans communicate with the spirit world. Tobacco was used medically. Some indigenous peoples believed tobacco could cure virtually everything, from bad breath and sore throats to poor vision and snakebites. The women of certain tribes drank tobacco tea to ease the pain of childbirth. In other tribes men dripped the juice from tobacco plants into their eyes before a hunt, believing

Throughout history, tobacco has been used for many different purposes, in many different ways, including in cigarettes and cigars.

this made their eyesight keener. The warriors of some tribes inhaled tobacco smoke before battles to make themselves fiercer. When food was scarce, some tribes even ate tobacco to stave off hunger.

Tobacco was also associated with cleansing and fertility. Tobacco smoke was blown onto women before marriage. This, it was believed, would promote fertility. Smoke was also blown over fields before planting to ensure a good harvest. And indigenous farmers used tobacco smoke to kill insects on their fruits and vegetables. (Nicotine is, in fact, a powerful insecticide.)

Spreading Northward

Many aspects of tobacco's early diffusion remain unknown. It is, for example, impossible to say precisely when or how tobacco arrived in a particular region because there is very little direct evidence. The earliest known depictions of tobacco use come from the Mayan civilization, which flourished in parts of present-day Honduras, Guatemala, Belize, and Mexico. Mayan stone carvings and painted pottery from the period AD 600–900 show rulers, gods, and priests smoking large cigars and even slender cigarettes. (The difference between a cigar and a cigarette isn't just the size. Cigars are rolled tobacco leaves; cigarettes consist of shredded tobacco inside a wrapper made from another material. Instead of paper wrappers, which are used today, the Mayans probably stuffed shredded tobacco in cornhusks or hollow reeds to make their cigarettes.)

Even though the Mayans first recorded scenes of tobacco use less than 1,500 years ago, tobacco spread through Central America and Mexico much earlier. N. rustica seeds found in a prehistoric site in New Mexico, the High Rolls Cave, prove that tobacco was already being grown in what is now the southwestern United

States by about 1000 BCE. Southwestern tribes cultivated tobacco in large gardens along with their major food crops—maize, beans, and squash.

From the Southwest, tobacco continued to spread north and east. By AD 800 at the latest, tobacco was being smoked by American Indian tribes all over North America except in the far north, where the climate made cultivating the plant impossible.

Most American Indian tribes smoked dried, crushed tobacco leaves in calumets—highly decorated pipes

In the southwestern United States, Native American tribes grew tobacco along with staple food crops like corn and beans.

made from stone, bone, clay, or wood. East Coast Indians even used lobster claws for pipe bowls. Some calumets depicted people or animals. When a person's face was carved on a pipe bowl, it was believed the smoker could communicate with that person. Waterfowl pipe carvings were popular because birds such as ducks or geese were thought to go into the three spiritual worlds of land, water, and air.

Food of the Spirits

Tobacco was believed to be the "food of the spirits," and the spirits seemed to have an endless hunger. Since they couldn't grow or eat it themselves, spirits depended on humans to deliver tobacco to them. Therefore, humans consumed tobacco during ritual offerings for the spirits. They believed the spirits would, in turn, bestow good favor and fortune on them.

When opposing groups of American Indians met, calumet rituals were held to help prevent warfare. Smoking together symbolized peaceful relations between potential enemies. Most agreements or treaties were not considered binding unless the ceremonial calumet or "peace pipe" was passed around. Peace pipes were also carried by messengers and guaranteed safe passage through hostile territory. Each tribe's pipes featured unique designs that were recognizable by members of other tribes.

Some tribes had several sets of smoking pipes. Among the Omaha people of the Great Plains, for example, men had one pipe for peace and one for war. The stems of the peace pipes were decorated with eagle feathers and duck skin. The war pipes, by contrast, had buzzard skin and feathers hanging from the stems.

American Indians did not typically smoke just for pleasure; they smoked with a purpose. Men of a tribe—in many cases only males were permitted to smoke—might light their pipes at specific times of the day, to communicate with the spirit world. Smoking was also customary at tribal councils convened to decide a particular issue. And sometimes men smoked as an act of friendship. When two members of the Karuk tribe of northern California met on a trail, for example, they would stop to smoke together before continuing on their separate ways.

Tobacco was smoked in pipes called calumets, which were made from stone, bone, clay, or wood and which were carved and decorated.

Tobacco Planters

Not all American Indian peoples established permanent villages. Plains Indians, for example, moved from one temporary camp to another throughout the year. Still, tribes such as the Blackfoot and the Crow planted tobacco along their migration routes. For them, tobacco meant existence or extinction. They believed that without the tobacco seed, leaf, and blossom, their nations would pass from the face of the earth.

The role of tobacco planter was therefore vital for these tribes. Candidates for the position had to endure extensive trials. They were cut, burned, and forced to go without food or water for days. If a man passed these tests, he traded all his earthly possessions for some tobacco seeds. Tobacco planters were believed to have supernatural powers to cure diseases, bring buffalo closer to camp, and even control the weather.

Tobacco Use Throughout the Americas

Tobacco was used in some fashion by almost all the cultures of the Americas. It was smoked in cigars, cigarettes, or pipes. It was chewed, sniffed through the nose, drunk in teas, or applied directly to the skin. It was used to cure people who were already sick and to protect people from future harm. Some cultures used tobacco as currency, as tokens of friendship, or as gifts.

Before the arrival of Europeans, tobacco may have been the most-traded crop in the Americas. Europeans, too, would come to prize the plant.

CHAPTER 2

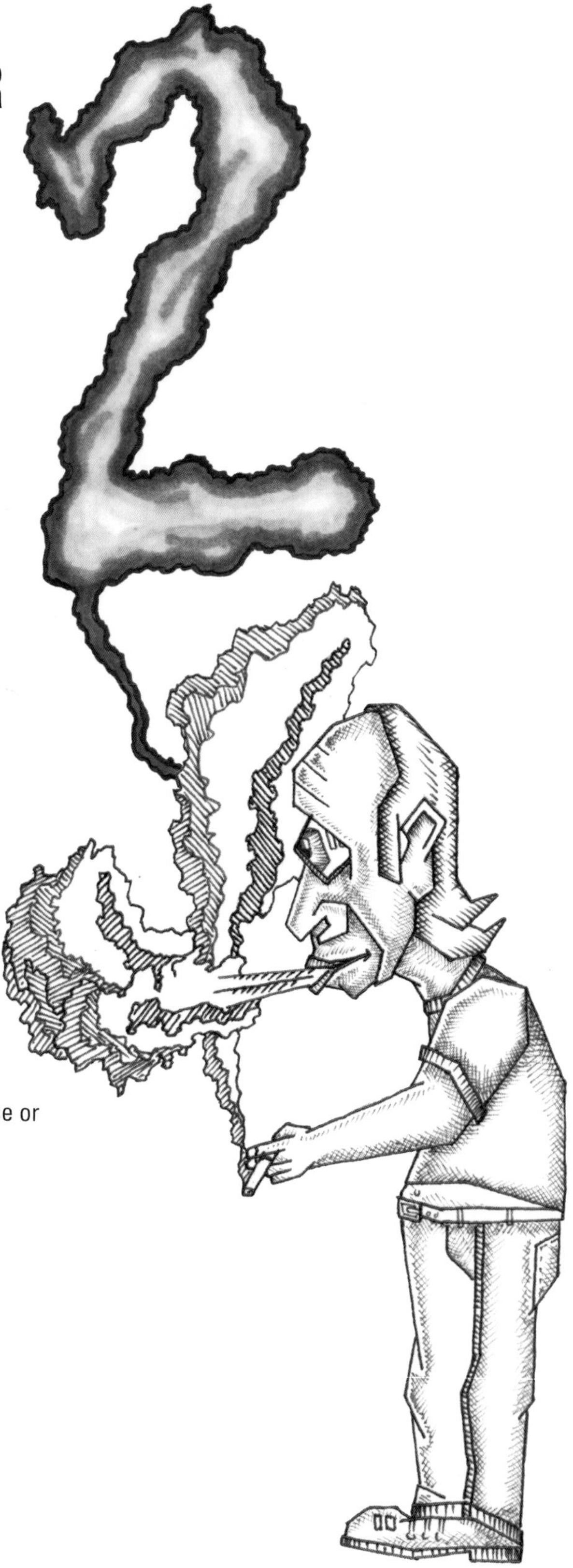

Words to Know

conquistador: A Spanish conqueror.

patrons: Regular customers.

prophylactic: Protecting against the occurrence of disease or infection.

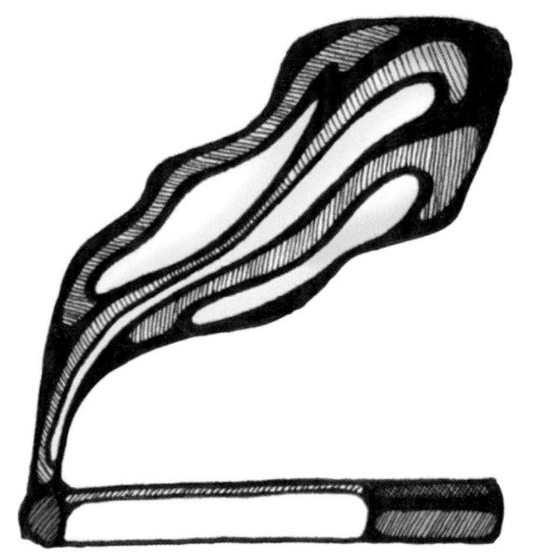

From the New World to the Old

The Americas introduced a number of important foods to the rest of the world: corn, potatoes, chocolate, tomatoes. But tobacco was the first product from the New World to conquer Europe.

When explorer Christopher Columbus set sail from Spain on August 3, 1492, he and his three ships were heading to China to trade for gold, silver, and silk. Until that time, bringing goods from the Orient to Europe involved a long and dangerous journey across the continent of Asia. Columbus believed he could find a better route by sailing west across the Atlantic Ocean. Of course, unbeknownst to him, the New World stood between him and China.

Columbus's ships first touched land in mid-October on the Bahamian island he named San Salvador. The natives were friendly and gave Columbus gifts of fruit and leaves. Columbus and his crew ate the fruit and tossed the ordinary-looking leaves overboard. From there, they sailed from island to island in the Caribbean. At each stop, Columbus and his crew received the puzzling gift of dried leaves.

Continuing westward, the sailors sighted a large landmass a few weeks later. It was the island of Cuba. Columbus assumed he had reached his intended destination. He sent two of his men ashore to arrange a meeting with the Chinese emperor.

While ashore, the men witnessed behavior they had never seen before. They reported to Columbus that the natives carried around musket-shaped rolls of dried herbs. They set one end on fire, and from the other end

Tobacco was introduced in Europe with Columbus' return to Spain after his "discovery" of the Americas.

they would suck or "drink" in the fragrant smoke. The natives invited the sailors to join them in smoking these dried herbs.

Return to the Old World

In March 1493, Columbus and his crew returned to Spain to tell King Ferdinand and Queen Isabella of their voyage. Columbus showed off his souvenirs, which included tobacco and a small amount of gold. He told of the strange custom of "drinking smoke."

On the return voyage to Spain, crewmember Rodrigo de Xerez had became hooked on tobacco. Citizens saw de Xerez around the waterfront and on the streets of Ayamonte, Spain, with smoke billowing from his nose and mouth. Spaniards had never seen such a thing. Many were certain that de Xerez was possessed by the devil.

Of Conquests and Tobacco

In the wake of Columbus's groundbreaking voyage, many Spanish adventurers and explorers sailed to the New World in search of gold and other riches. Spanish colonies were established on the islands of Hispaniola, Cuba, and Puerto Rico.

In 1519, the *conquistador* Hernán Cortés led an expedition to the mainland. Cortés and his men landed on the east coast of Mexico, then marched and fought their way inland to Tenochtitlán, capital of the powerful Aztec Empire. There the conquistadors seized the Aztec leader, Montezuma II, and held him for a ransom of his empire's gold.

The conquistadors lived in Montezuma's palace and shared meals with their captive. After one such meal, the Aztec emperor lit a very unusual cigar: it was in a gilded, painted tube.

Cortés and other members of his expedition tried tobacco. So did Spanish and Portuguese explorers and

Tobacco use was an important part of the cultural exchange between the New World and the Old.

soldiers who followed. Many became addicted. When they returned to Spain and Portugal, some of these adventurers brought back private stashes of tobacco to feed their cravings. Before long, the sight of sailors spewing tobacco smoke had become commonplace.

Eventually the explorers began to return to their homelands with more than dried tobacco leaves. By the 1550s, they had brought back tobacco seeds. In Spain and Portugal, royal households grew tobacco plants as ornamental shrubbery in their palace gardens. As news of these new plants spread in Europe, representatives of royal families from surrounding countries asked for cuttings of the new exotic plant. They wanted to grow tobacco for decoration on their estates, too.

France Joins the Tobacco Craze

In the late 1550s a French ambassador, Jean Nicot, traveled to Portugal. His mission was to arrange a royal marriage, but while in Portugal, Nicot obtained some tobacco plants. He wasn't just interested in growing tobacco for ornamental purposes, however. Nicot had heard rumors that tobacco held healing powers,

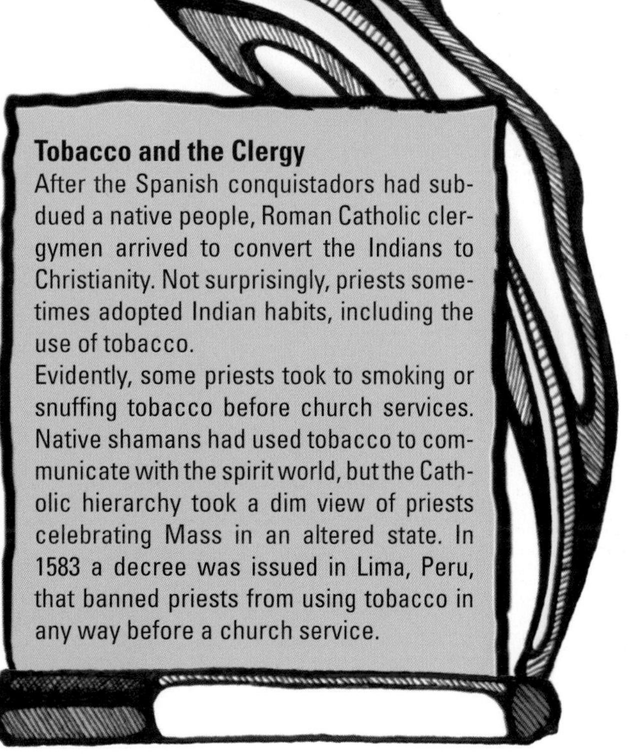

Tobacco and the Clergy

After the Spanish conquistadors had subdued a native people, Roman Catholic clergymen arrived to convert the Indians to Christianity. Not surprisingly, priests sometimes adopted Indian habits, including the use of tobacco.

Evidently, some priests took to smoking or snuffing tobacco before church services. Native shamans had used tobacco to communicate with the spirit world, but the Catholic hierarchy took a dim view of priests celebrating Mass in an altered state. In 1583 a decree was issued in Lima, Peru, that banned priests from using tobacco in any way before a church service.

Catherine de Medici started the tobacco fad in Europe when she began using snuff and tobacco leaves to alleviate headaches.

and he made an ointment of the leaves. According to legend, a Lisbon man rubbed the ointment on his cancerous tumor and was soon cured.

When Nicot returned to Paris in 1561, he showed the tobacco to Queen Catherine de Medici. He told her of his experiments with tobacco ointments for external wounds. Nicot also told her that tobacco was taken as snuff for internal ailments. The queen was intrigued. She began taking snuff and applying tobacco leaves to her forehead to relieve migraine headaches. When word of this spread, wealthy people in Paris also began using tobacco for medical purposes.

Jean Nicot was celebrated for his discoveries. Both the genus Nicotiana and nicotine, the addictive substance found in tobacco, would be named for him.

Tobacco "Vitamins"

Between 1565 and 1574, Nicolás Monardes—a doctor from Seville, Spain—published a three-part encyclopedia that detailed the healing properties of plants and other products of the New World. Among them was tobacco. Like Native American shamans, Monardes believed that tobacco could cure a broad range of ailments, including internal illnesses, kidney stones, toothaches, and bad breath. His work was translated into several languages, and word of this miracle substance—tobacco—spread throughout Europe.

Soon tobacco was being taken as a *prophylactic*, similar

Animal Cure-All

Doctor Nicolás Monardes from Seville, Spain, not only suggested using tobacco as a cure for almost any human ailment; he believed the plant would cure animals, too. Monardes said tobacco could cure cattle's wounds, infections, hoof-and-mouth disease, and parasites.

Sir Walter Raleigh would hand out pipes and pouches of tobacco to Londoners in an attempt to make tobacco catch on.

to how people today use vitamins. In many cases addiction resulted. It was said that some people would rather snuff tobacco than eat.

Wealthy Europeans began growing their own tobacco for personal use. But it wasn't as good or as strong as the tobacco grown in the Americas. Demand for tobacco from the Americas grew. Spanish and Portuguese ships began bringing back more tobacco to fill this demand. But this imported tobacco was very expensive. Spain set up plantations in the Caribbean. Tobacco had become an international business.

The Appetite for Tobacco Grows

Before long, tobacco use expanded to Italy, Germany, Switzerland, and Holland. The market for tobacco seemed almost limitless.

Tobacco had found its way to England in 1565, when slave traders brought some back from Florida. But the person most responsible for the growth of tobacco's popularity in England was the explorer Sir Walter Raleigh. Raleigh regaled Queen Elizabeth I with his stories of tobacco's medicinal uses and alluring qualities, smoking his pipe all the while. Elizabeth and her court began smoking tobacco in small "elfin" pipes.

In a clever marketing ploy, Raleigh also handed out pouches of tobacco and armloads of pipes to the crowds at London's famed Mermaid Tavern. The *patrons* enjoyed smoking tobacco, and word soon spread about this new pastime. Before long, English citizens were smoking tobacco everywhere—from the courtroom to the theater, in city parks, and while traveling to and from church. Plays, poems, and books were written about smoking, and pipe smoking became England's most popular leisure activity.

Spain quickly developed a monopoly on tobacco, since it had many colonies in the Americas, whereas England had to rely on trade and plunder to get tobacco.

Unlike Spain, however, England lacked colonies in the Americas at this time. Thus it had nowhere to grow fine-quality tobacco to satisfy its growing domestic demand. And during the late sixteenth century, England and Spain were at war, making it difficult to obtain tobacco through trade. Most of the tobacco consumed in England came from captured Spanish ships.

From the British point of view, plundering Spanish shipping might have seemed an ideal way to supply English smokers with the tobacco they craved. Certainly it was easier and cheaper than setting up British colonies in the Americas. But there was one huge problem: a sufficient and steady supply of tobacco could never be guaranteed, because chance played a great role in how many Spanish ships were seized in any given period. So sometimes there would be a lot of tobacco for the British market, whereas other times virtually none would be available. This kept the cost of tobacco in England very high. England's situation, however, was about to change.

CHAPTER

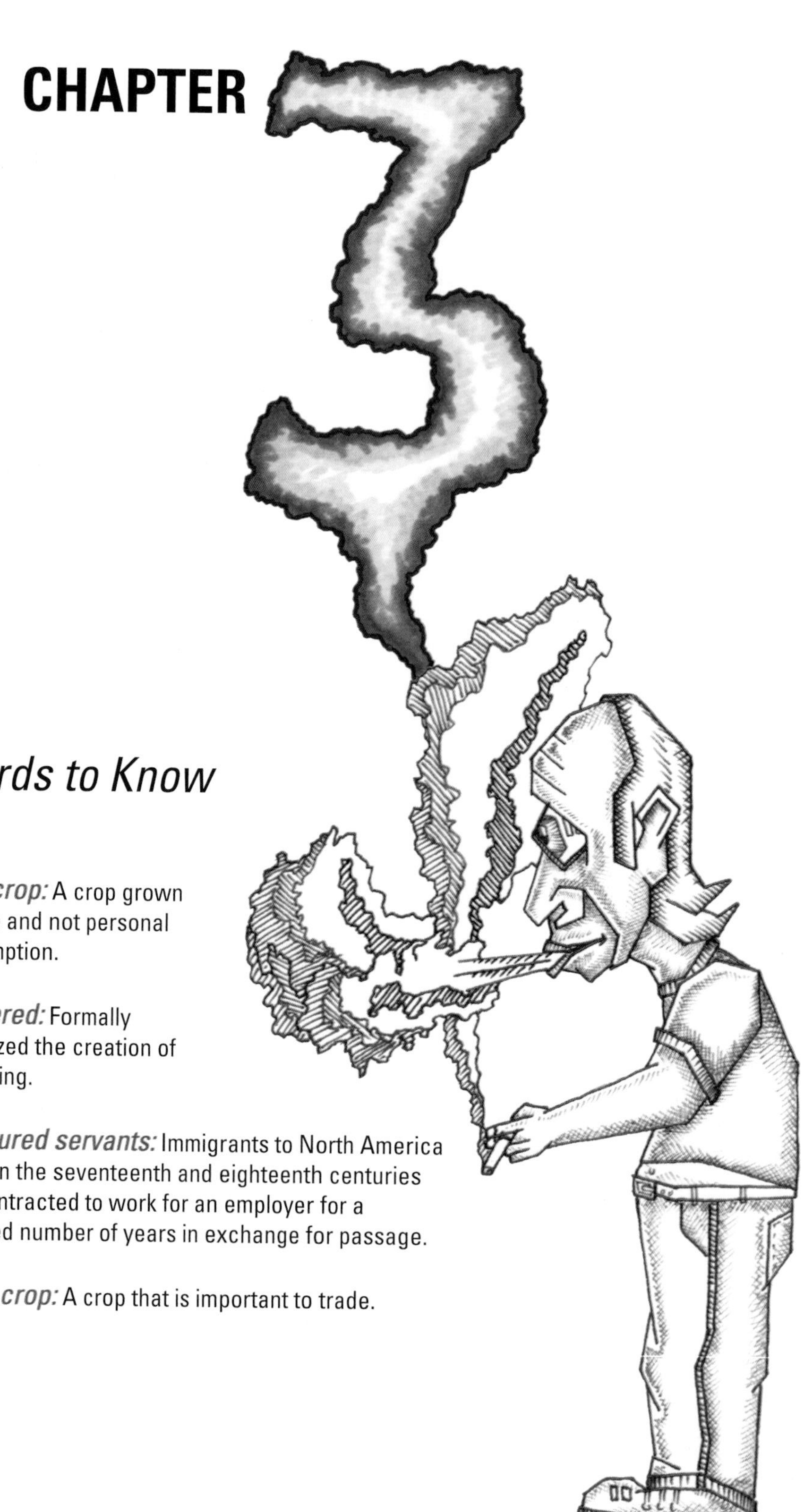

Words to Know

cash crop: A crop grown for sale and not personal consumption.

chartered: Formally authorized the creation of something.

indentured servants: Immigrants to North America between the seventeenth and eighteenth centuries who contracted to work for an employer for a specified number of years in exchange for passage.

staple crop: A crop that is important to trade.

How Tobacco Saved Colonial America

In 1606 King James I chartered an *investment* group, the Virginia Company, to establish a British colony in North America. Three ships carrying a total of more than one hundred settlers sailed from England in December. By May 1607 the men had arrived in the New World and selected a site for their settlement along a river emptying into the Chesapeake Bay. In honor of their king, they named the river the James and the settlement Jamestown.

The colonists had heard tales of what to expect in the New World. Unfortunately, the stories weren't exactly accurate. They landed expecting to see the ground covered with gold

An early illustration of the tobacco industry in Colonial America showing various steps in the process.

nuggets and jewels, theirs for the taking. But instead of easy riches, they found a lot of hard work. These men were not well versed in survival skills. While they were able to get some food by trading with the local Powhatan tribe, conditions were grim. By the end of the first winter, malnutrition, disease, exposure, and Indian attacks had claimed the lives of all but 38 of the original 104 colonists.

Try, Try Again

Despite the problems encountered by the first settlers to the region, more Englishmen came to Jamestown. To prove that Jamestown could be a worthwhile investment, the colonists tried to come up with a profitable product to ship back to the mother country. They made glass, wine, and beer for export. Unfortunately, people back in England weren't interested in any of those items. So colonists tried growing the local strain of tobacco, *Nicotiana rustica*. However, that tobacco had a more bitter taste than the Caribbean-grown *Nicotiana tabacum* variety people in England were used to. It appeared that the Jamestown colony would fail.

Near hopelessness, the colonist John Rolfe asked a friend to bring back some *N. tabacum* seeds from the island of Trinidad. Rolfe planted the seeds in 1612. His first crop of tobacco was disappointing, but he didn't give up. Instead, he experimented with the growing, blending, and curing processes of tobacco. Rolfe got tips from the Caribbean tobacco growers and from the family of his Indian wife, Pocahontas. After a few years, he finally came up with a unique, mild-flavored tobacco.

In 1615 and 1616, Rolfe shipped a total of 2,300 pounds of tobacco leaves to England. The English loved the new Virginian tobacco blend and demanded more of the "brown gold." The price of Virginia tobacco shot up. This was the boost Jamestown needed.

Everyone Grew Tobacco

Word of Rolfe's success electrified the Jamestown colonists. He shared his seeds, and soon others were growing tobacco as a cash crop. In fact, colonists were so excited about the prospect of making huge profits from tobacco that many stopped growing food crops. Reminding the colonists that they couldn't eat money, colonial governor Thomas Dale decreed that for every acre of tobacco they planted, colonists had to plant two acres of corn. Unfortunately, Dale's decree was ignored. By 1617 tobacco grew everywhere, even in the streets.

Producing tobacco, while it could be very profitable, wasn't easy. After tilling and planting their fields, colonists had to water, weed, remove insects, prune, harvest, dry, cure, shred, pack, and store their tobacco before it could be sold. It was a labor-intensive process. Some growers used *indentured servants* to help in the fields, but there weren't enough servants to go around.

A Change on the Horizon

In 1619 a Dutch trading ship arrived in Jamestown and changed everything. The governor and a merchant bought twenty black slaves from the Dutch ship in exchange for some Virginia tobacco and other supplies. These slaves were put to work in tobacco fields. Soon other tobacco growers bought additional slaves to work in their fields.

Slave labor enabled more land to be cultivated and helped lead to a dramatic jump in tobacco production. About 50,000 pounds of tobacco were exported in 1618, the year before the first slaves arrived. In 1639, the Virginia colony exported 1.5 million pounds.

Golden Token

Tobacco became more than just a crop; it became a form of currency. "Golden tokens," or tobacco leaves, varied in value. In years when tobacco was plentiful, the leaves were worth less. When years of drought decreased the quantity of available tobacco, the leaves were worth more. This was the economic law of supply and demand in action.

In colonial America, tobacco was used as currency and a person's wealth was measured in how much tobacco he had.

A man's wealth was measured in the amount of tobacco he had. Colonists used tobacco as currency to buy merchandise and more slaves, pay their taxes, and even to transport wives. In 1621, a group of men each paid 120 pounds of tobacco leaves for a ship to bring wives over from England.

Tobacco was at the center of almost every transaction within the colony, as well as between the colony and the outside world. Colonists who didn't grow tobacco, such as the blacksmith, saddle maker, or clergyman, traded their services for tobacco, with which they in turn bought the things they needed.

The Tobacco Region Grows

Tobacco could only be grown in the same field for four to seven years before the soil was depleted of nutrients. And it took almost twenty years for the soil quality to

While tobacco cultivation began in Virginia, soon the crop had spread throughout the thirteen colonies, becoming an important crop all over the New World.

recover. That was obviously too long for tobacco growers to wait. Growers could have rotated crops, planting tobacco in their fields for a few years and then switching to a food crop for a year or two to restore the soil. Instead, they grew tobacco until a plot of land was exhausted, then simply moved on to another plot of land to plant more tobacco.

This was possible because land was cheap, if not free, and slavery provided a source of low-cost labor for the backbreaking work of chopping down trees and clearing vegetation. Large plantations developed, and some Virginia planters became extremely wealthy.

Eventually, tobacco growing spread beyond Virginia into the neighboring colonies of Maryland and North Carolina. By the 1730s, tobacco had become a *staple crop* throughout the thirteen British colonies in North America.

Early Quality Control

In 1730 the Virginia colony instituted a law called the Virginia Inspection Act. It required that all tobacco be taken to a public warehouse for inspection before it was sold. Public officials inspected each hogshead, which was between eight hundred and one thousand pounds of tobacco, to make sure it was free from trash and dirt. Tobacco that wasn't up to the standards was destroyed. This prevented low-quality tobacco from entering the English market. The quality-control idea spread, and the colony of Maryland created a similar inspection system in 1747.

If a grower's tobacco passed inspection, he received a note indicating the weight of his tobacco. If a man didn't have enough tobacco to fill a whole hogshead, he received a transfer note for the amount he turned in. These notes were used like currency to buy things or pay off a debt.

England's Piece of the Pie

Tobacco exports to England may have made some colonial planters wealthy, but over the years the relationship between the colonists and the mother country became strained. The British government believed it had the right to control trade with the colonies. For example, it taxed tobacco exports from the colonies, dictated the price of colonial tobacco, and prohibited the colonists from selling their tobacco to other European nations, such as France.

Soldiers who fought in the Revolutionary War were often paid with tobacco; the amount depended on their rank.

Many colonists considered these policies unfair, and they found ways around the rules. For example, they smuggled tobacco into other countries or bribed officials responsible for collecting export taxes.

Tobacco and the Revolution

On April 19, 1775, colonists and British soldiers exchanged fire in Lexington and Concord, Massachusetts. The Revolutionary War had begun, and the colonists' trade with England stopped. With no more exports to England, there was a surplus of tobacco leaves, and colonists came up with creative ways to use their stockpiles.

Soldiers were paid with tobacco. The amount of tobacco they received depended on their rank. When a man died on the battlefield, his fellow soldiers smoked his pipe or cigar as a memorial to their fallen comrade.

When civilians asked General George Washington—the commander in chief of the Continental Army, the army of the thirteen colonies—how they could help with the war effort, he told them that if they couldn't contribute money, they should send tobacco. The thirteen colonies used tobacco not only to pay their soldiers' salaries but also to buy food, clothing, and guns.

The "Tobacco War"

The Revolutionary War dragged on for years. Neither the British nor the Americans were able to win a decisive victory on the battlefield.

In 1780 and 1781, the British strategy focused on winning in the southern colonies. As part of this effort, British generals Cornwallis, Phillips, and Arnold launched a campaign called the "Tobacco War." Determined to make the rebellious colonists pay a steep economic price, the British seized and destroyed 10,000 hogsheads of

Tobacco plantations required a huge amount of manpower to run. Because of this, indentured servants, and later slaves, were often used on these large farms.

tobacco in Virginia. They burned colonists' curing barns and tobacco fields, and they freed colonists' slaves. Some of the Virginia tobacco destroyed by Cornwallis's men belonged to Thomas Jefferson, the author of the Declaration of Independence. Jefferson called the torching of his tobacco "a useless and barbarous injury."

In the end, the British efforts failed. In October 1781, Cornwallis surrendered a large British force at Yorktown, Virginia. Though a peace treaty wouldn't be signed for two more years, the major fighting had ended. The United States had won independence from Britain.

To the American colonists, tobacco was more than just a crop. In many ways, it was a symbol of America. After the Revolutionary War, as Americans pushed further west across the continent, they took tobacco with them.

Indentured to Tobacco

Before 1680, indentured servants provided most of the labor needed to work the fields for tobacco growers. According to some sources, as many as one-half to two-thirds of all immigrants to the New World from England and Ireland in the 1600s were indentured servants. Over 100,000 poor, unskilled young men and women exchanged four to seven years of hard work for their fare to the New World. The majority of them worked in the tobacco fields.

Once indentured servants' terms of service were up, they were free to start afresh. Many of them purchased land, built homes, and continued to grow tobacco.

The supply of indentured servants dwindled by the end of the 1600s. By 1670, each tobacco grower averaged

In many ways, tobacco plantations like this one served as the center of the colonies' economy; tobacco was considered a currency, even when it came to paying clergy.

1.75 servants and .25 slaves per tobacco farm. Slaves cost the grower two and a half times more than indentured servants did, but slaves' service was for a lifetime, not just a few years.

Tobacco Preachers

Colonists in Virginia used their tobacco leaves like currency around town and in church. They paid their preachers with tobacco. The men of the cloth didn't mind getting paid in tobacco leaves. A Virginia clergyman's average salary in the 1690s was about 16,000 pounds of good leaf. A preacher could supplement his salary by charging extra for special ceremonies like weddings.

CHAPTER 4

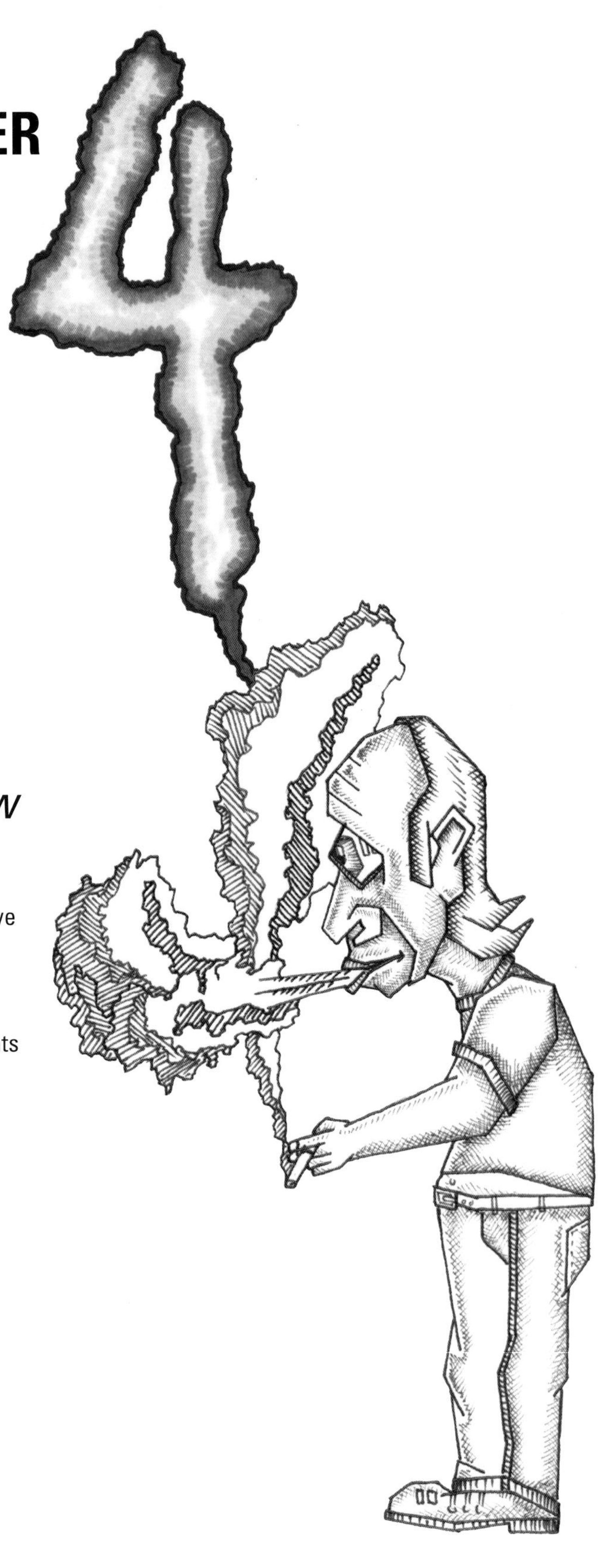

Words to Know

migrants: People who move from one place to another, often for work.

squatters: Illegal occupants of land.

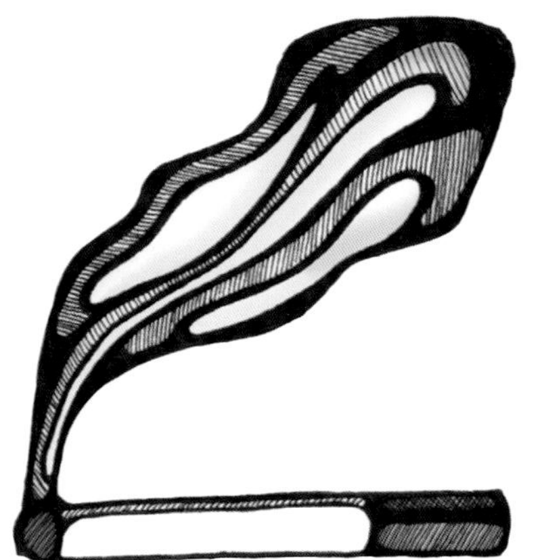

Westward Ho

American growers didn't export much tobacco during the war years; most was kept for domestic consumption. After Americans gained their independence, they smoked more tobacco than ever before. They smoked as they pushed inland from the "Tobacco Coast" into the wilderness of the new nation.

Many *migrants* set up their homesteads on the frontier as *squatters*. They cleared the land, built their homes, and grew crops to feed their families. When it came time to stake their claim, many didn't have enough money to have their land surveyed, because they didn't have an income. Owners of large plantations often paid squatters' survey fees, then booted them off the land and took over their farms.

Most plantation owners had shifted to growing grains and raising cattle to survive during the Revolutionary War, since less tobacco was sent abroad. Those activities were not as labor intensive as growing tobacco, so fewer slaves were needed. Many tobacco growers sold off their slaves to owners of cotton plantations.

Cigars' Popularity Grows

Israel Putnam, a general in the Continental Army during the Revolutionary War, had previously spent some time in Cuba. There Putnam had been introduced to Cuban cigars. Putnam brought three mule loads of Cuban cigars back to his home in Connecticut. He kept some of the cigars for himself and sold others. They were very popular, and Putnam became America's first importer of Cuban cigars.

Americans tried making their own cigars. Tobacco seeds were brought from Cuba to grow tobacco for this purpose. One factory in South Windsor, Connecticut, began making cigars in 1801. They were cheaper than Cuban cigars, but they weren't as good. Another company rolled cigars in Conestoga, Pennsylvania. Its product, Conestogas ("stogies"), became a favorite of migrants heading west.

Louisiana Purchase Opens the Doors to the West

At the beginning of the nineteenth century, France was embroiled in a costly war with other European countries. In need of money with which to fund his army, the French leader, Napoleon Bonaparte, decided to sell the Louisiana Territory to the United States for $15

While cigars originally came from Cuba, it wasn't long before Americans tried making their own.

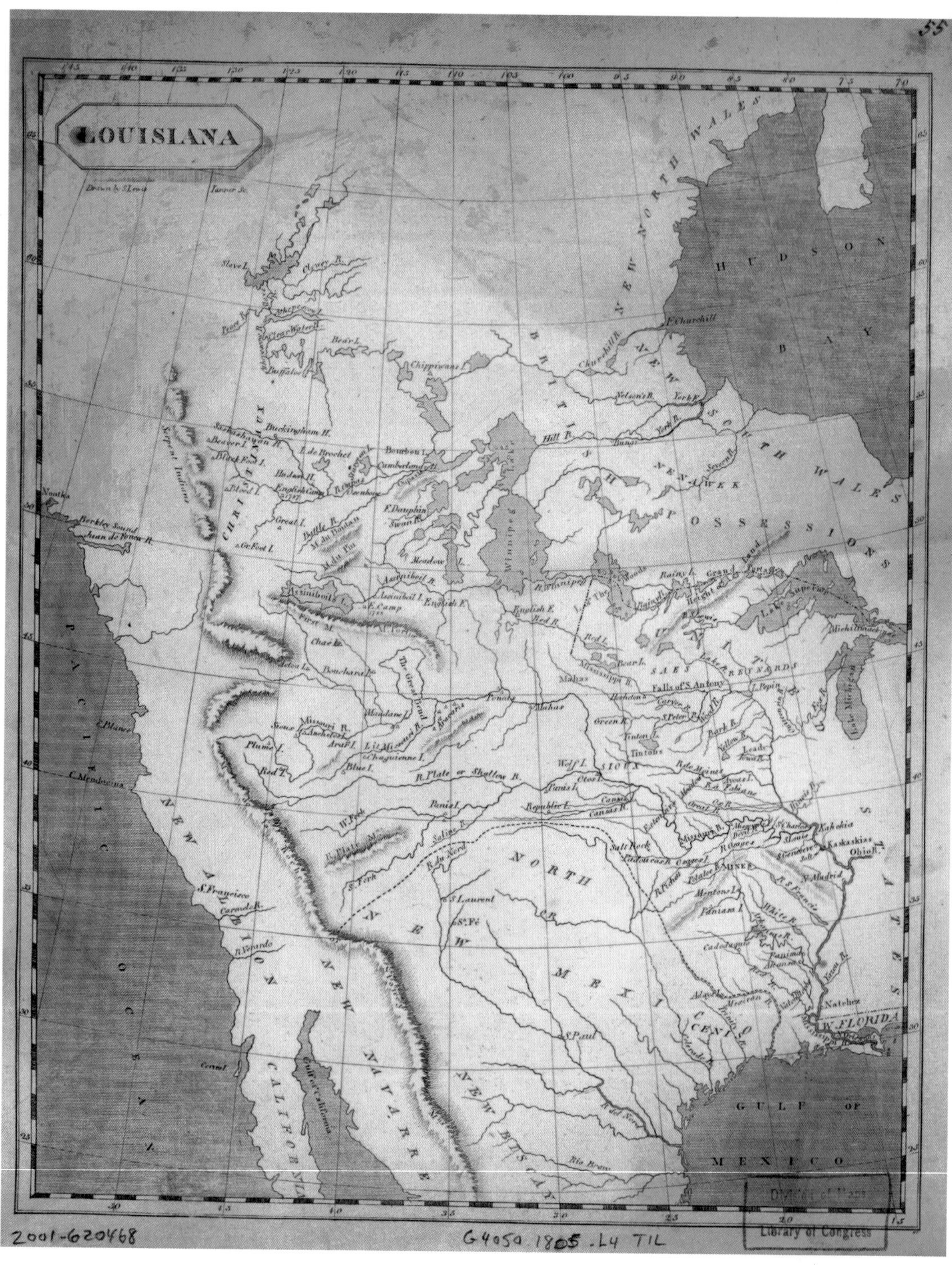

The Louisiana Purchase doubled the size of the United States.

million. Extending from the Mississippi River to the Rocky Mountains, this enormous chunk of land covered 828,000 square miles. On April 30, 1803, negotiators from the United States and France signed the Louisiana Purchase. At a cost of less than five cents an acre, the United States doubled its size. The purchase opened the door for U.S. expansion to the Pacific coast.

Thomas Jefferson, the third president of the United States, decided to dispatch an expedition to explore the Louisiana Territory and find a route to the Pacific Ocean. Two men, Captain Meriwether Lewis and Captain Wil-

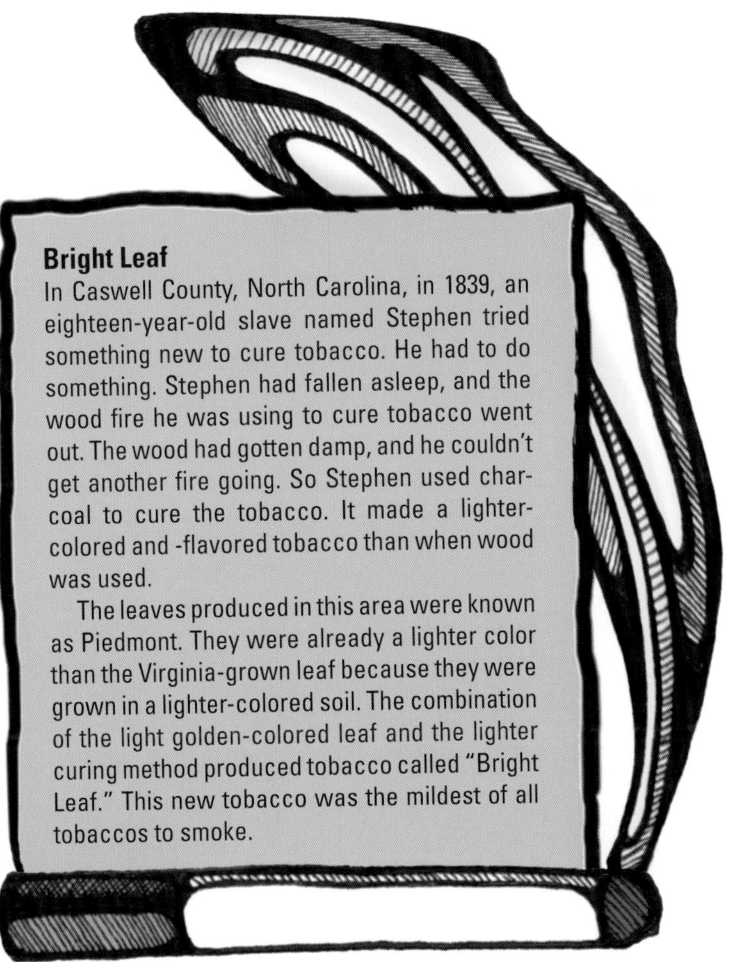

Bright Leaf

In Caswell County, North Carolina, in 1839, an eighteen-year-old slave named Stephen tried something new to cure tobacco. He had to do something. Stephen had fallen asleep, and the wood fire he was using to cure tobacco went out. The wood had gotten damp, and he couldn't get another fire going. So Stephen used charcoal to cure the tobacco. It made a lighter-colored and -flavored tobacco than when wood was used.

The leaves produced in this area were known as Piedmont. They were already a lighter color than the Virginia-grown leaf because they were grown in a lighter-colored soil. The combination of the light golden-colored leaf and the lighter curing method produced tobacco called "Bright Leaf." This new tobacco was the mildest of all tobaccos to smoke.

Chewing tobacco became increasingly popular in the 1800s.

liam Clark, would lead the expedition, called the Corps of Discovery. Lewis was a keen observer of plants and animals, while Clark had remarkable mapmaking skills. The Corps of Discovery, consisting of more than 40 men, set off from St. Louis on May 14, 1804. The men headed up the Missouri River.

Lewis and Clark filled their boats with essential food, clothing, tents, arms, and twists of tobacco, among other supplies. They planned to use the tobacco to trade and smoke with Native Americans as a gesture of friendship. When they passed through tribe's territory, they gave the chief a friendship medallion and several twists of tobacco. Tobacco served as the Corps' passport for the next two years, getting them safely through dangerous territories.

Unfortunately, Lewis didn't account for tobacco's popularity among his own men. Not long into the journey, it became clear that he would have to ration the men's tobacco. This was difficult since the men craved it. As a treat, Lewis and Clark distributed a few tobacco twists to the men at Christmas. This may have been the men's best Christmas gift ever.

To stretch out the Virginia tobacco, they added leaves and bark of bearberry, wild crabapple, or red willow plants. One of the men, Sergeant Patrick Gass, wrote in his journal on March 7, 1806 (as quoted on the Web site LewisandClarkTrail.com), "Among our other difficulties we now experience the want of tobacco, and out of 33 persons composing our party, there are but 7 who do not make use of it; we use crab-tree bark as a substitute."

When the men's stock of tobacco ran out, they tried the local "Indian tobacco," *Nicotiana quadrivalvis*. It didn't have the same flavor as the Virginian variety they were used to, and though it was tolerable to smoke, it wasn't very good to chew. Most men in the Corps preferred to chew tobacco instead of smoke it.

The Corps reached the Pacific in late 1805. The following spring, the men headed for home. They finally reached St. Louis on September 23, 1806. After months without decent tobacco, the men were overjoyed to get all the Virginia-grown tobacco they wanted.

Lewis and Clark reported their findings to President Jefferson, and they also published the results of their journey to the Pacific. The expedition helped inspire thousands of Americans to look to the west.

In the decades that followed the journey of the Corps of Discovery, Americans pushed the country's frontier steadily west. And the westward migrants brought tobacco with them.

Smokeless Chewing Tobacco

Chewing tobacco, or "chaw," became an increasingly popular way for Americans to enjoy tobacco, particularly on the frontier. Companies created chaw by soaking cured tobacco leaves in large tubs with a sweetener and flavorings. The "weed soup" was then poured into molds to dry. The dried blocks were cut by hand into one-inch-diameter rods known as "plugs." Customers bought lengths of plug from stores.

Tobacco chewers carved off a piece of plug with a knife, then chewed it for a few minutes to soften it up. The chaw was then tucked between their cheek and gums. The tobacco's flavoring increased saliva production. Each piece of chaw lasted about an hour and produced about a cup of saliva. To avoid getting sick, the chewer needed to spit out the brown saliva instead of swallowing it. Chewing became a national pastime, and spittoons were so prevalent they could have become a national symbol. Unfortunately, many tobacco chewers were not great shots, and an unattractive

Recipe for Success

The formula for chewing tobacco was a guarded secret in each factory making it in the 1830s. Lists of ingredients may have given the impression that cake, rather than a tobacco product, was being made. The tobacco was soaked in vats of flavorings before it was pressed into molds. Most chewing tobacco included a sweetener such as molasses, sugar, or honey. Some contained up to 25 percent sugar. Sweeteners were combined with flavors such as licorice, rum, nutmeg, tonka beans, cinnamon, almond oil, lemon, cardamom, mace, caraway, and fennel seed.

Chewing tobacco had masculine-sounding brand names such as Live and Let Live, Buzz Saw, Barbed Wire, Bull of the Woods, and Cannon Ball.

and unhealthy coat of brown tobacco spit became a common sight across the nation.

Tobacco in the Civil War

The Civil War (1861–1865) was a gut-wrenching time in American history. The conflict—which claimed more American lives than any other war in history—pitted the North (the Union) against the South (the Confederacy). At issue was whether slavery would continue and whether states had the right to secede, or withdraw, from the United States.

Men smoked more during the war than ever before, to relieve stress and as a social activity. Commanders encouraged their men to smoke; it distracted them from the horrors of the war. One of the Civil War's most famous smokers, Ulysses S. Grant, always had a cigar in his mouth. Grant, commander of the Union forces, chewed on the cigar as he addressed his men, strolled

Spittoons like this one were placed outside of public places to allow people to spit their tobacco-filled saliva somewhere.

During the Civil War, smoking became both a way to relieve stress and to socialize with others.

around camp, or rode his horse. Grant often went into battle with an unlit cigar clenched in his teeth. He waited for a sure victory before he lit it. He was so famous for his cigar smoking that people sent him more cigars than he could smoke in a lifetime.

To help fund the war, the U.S. government began taxing tobacco. The government taxed factories based on the pounds of goods they produced. The tax jumped from five to forty cents per pound by war's end. The government also taxed consumers four cents for each nickel cigar they bought. In 1862, the first government tax on tobacco added about $3 million to the Treasury's coffers.

The 1800s saw tobacco used in many ways—smoked in pipes, rolled into cigars, and chewed. But there was another tobacco product on the horizon, one that would change how America and the world consumed tobacco. That was the cigarette.

CHAPTER 5

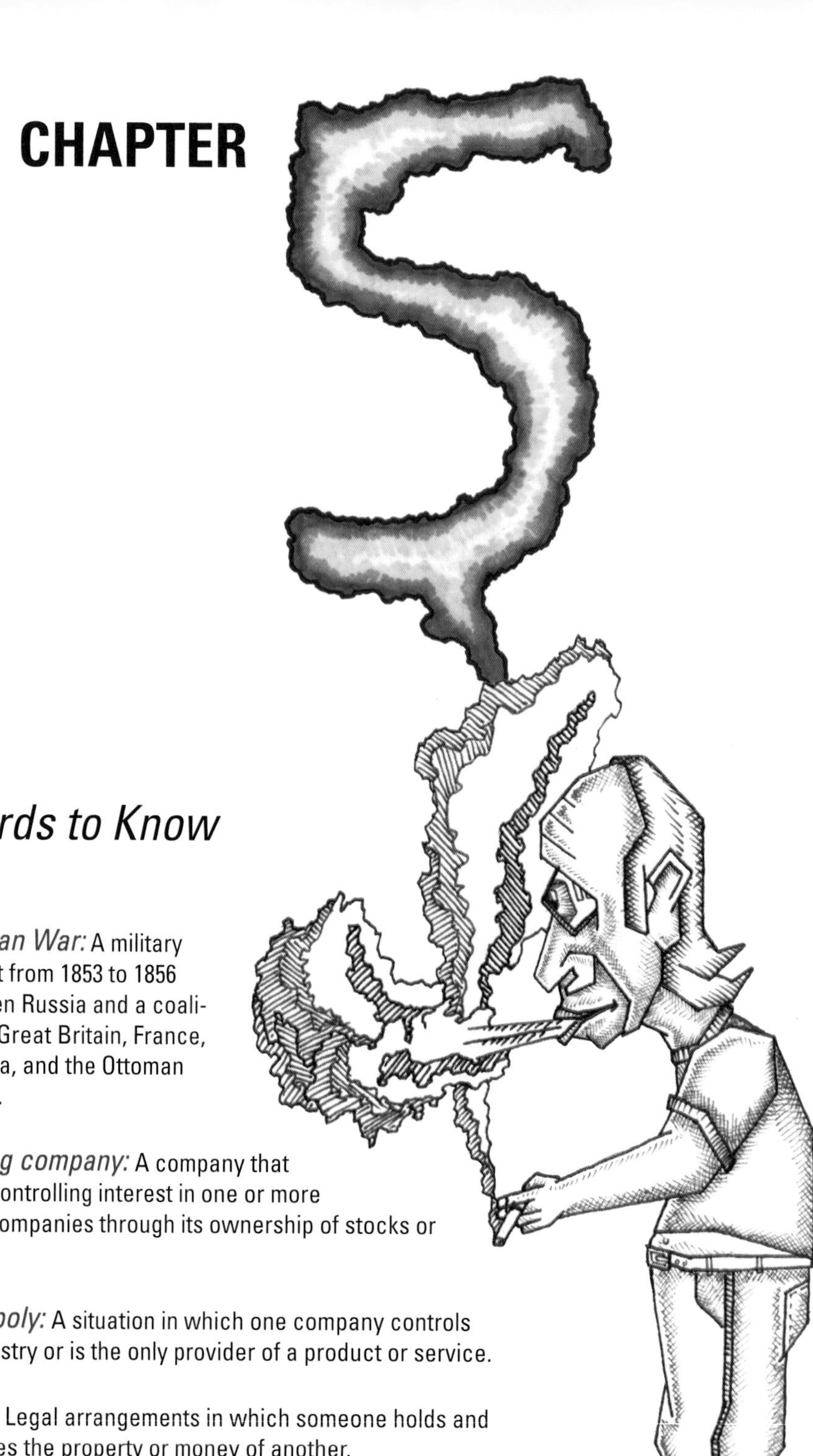

Words to Know

Crimean War: A military conflict from 1853 to 1856 between Russia and a coalition of Great Britain, France, Sardinia, and the Ottoman Empire.

holding company: A company that has a controlling interest in one or more other companies through its ownership of stocks or bonds.

monopoly: A situation in which one company controls an industry or is the only provider of a product or service.

trusts: Legal arrangements in which someone holds and manages the property or money of another.

Cigarette Mass Production

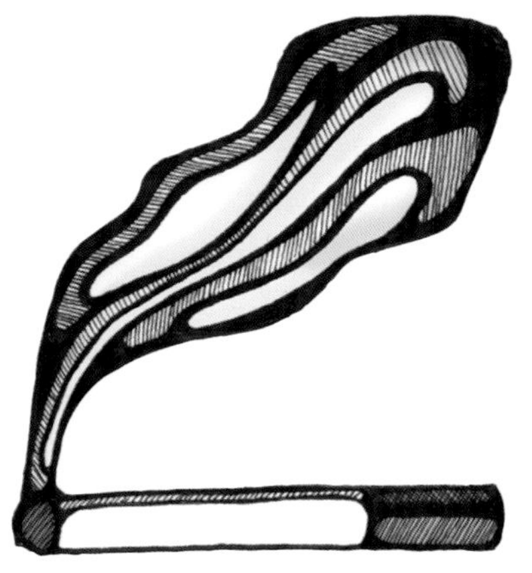

Indigenous peoples of South America and Central America smoked a form of cigarettes. They wrapped maize husks around loose tobacco or stuffed loose tobacco into hollow reeds to create their cigarettes. But cigarette smoking was slow to catch on with Europeans, and with citizens of the United States.

In Europe, very poor and homeless people probably began gathering tobacco from discarded cigar butts and pipe scrapings. They placed the tobacco onto a piece of paper, rolled it up, and smoked it. In the 1600s in Seville, Spain, a manufacturer made "poor man's cigars," or cigarettes, using leftover tobacco from the cigar industry.

But the spread of cigarettes across Europe and to England began only in the 1850s, with the *Crimean War*. From England cigarettes made their way across the Atlantic to the United States right before the Civil War. Their small size made cigarettes easy for soldiers to carry around on the battlefield. It also took less time to smoke a cigarette than a pipe or a cigar. In addition, cigarettes packed a nicotine punch of 9 to 10 percent, compared to 2 percent with a cigar and even less for pipe and chewing tobacco. This extra nicotine helped battle-weary soldiers stay alert.

The Automated Cigarette Machine

After the Civil War, cigarettes became popular with consumers in the United States. They were easier to light and stayed lit longer than cigars or pipes. Americans smoked cigarettes in such large quantities that factories couldn't keep up with demand. Cigarettes were made by

Before the invention of the cigarette rolling machine, cigarettes were rolled by hand in family homes like this one.

hand—a tedious process. Expert cigarette rollers could only make about three cigarettes per minute. Cigarette companies needed a million rollers to make enough cigarettes for all their customers. In the 1870s, nine-tenths of cigarette production costs went to pay the rollers. To increase profits and satisfy growing demand, cigarette production needed to be automated.

In 1875 the leading U.S. cigarette manufacturer, Allen & Ginter, of Richmond, Virginia, offered a prize of $75,000 to the person who could invent a cigarette-making machine. In 1880 James Albert Bonsack, the twenty-one-year-old son of a plantation owner, obtained a patent for his invention for just such a machine. Shredded tobacco was poured into one end of the machine, and a single long tube of paper-covered tobacco came out the other. These tubes were then automatically cut into uniform lengths. Bonsack claimed his machine could make 70,000 cigarettes per day. Allen & Ginter installed the machine but soon rejected it, saying it didn't work as promised. The company didn't pay Bonsack the prize money either.

The Duke Dynasty

James "Buck" Duke of W. Duke, Sons & Company of Durham, North Carolina, heard of Bonsack's invention. He bought two of Bonsack's machines and had them installed in his factory, where the company's mechanic fine-tuned them. On the first day of production, April 30, 1884, one machine produced 120,000 cigarettes in a ten-hour day. That was as many cigarettes as sixty skilled rollers could make in the same amount of time. Bonsack's machine only needed three men to run it: two men to feed in the cured tobacco and one to operate the machine. The era of modern cigarettes was born.

Duke's competitors quickly jumped on the bandwagon and purchased Bonsack's machines for their factories. Before long, machine-made cigarettes flooded the market. America's cigarette production went from nine million in 1885 to sixty million just two years later. With so many cigarettes produced with cheaper labor costs, part of the savings was passed along to the customers, making cigarettes available to average citizens at an affordable price.

Every Trick in the Book

Even though some of Duke's competitors had Bonsack's machines, they were not producing and selling as many cigarettes as W. Duke, Sons & Company. By 1889 Duke sold two million cigarettes a day, making it the top cigarette manufacturer in America.

It was important for Buck Duke to make his company's name recognizable. That way people would ask specifically for Duke's cigarettes instead of a competitor's. Previously, people

World's Rarest Baseball Card

Honus Wagner was a shortstop for the Pittsburgh Pirates baseball team from 1900 to 1917. In 1909 he didn't want his picture on a cigarette trading card produced by the American Tobacco Company. Why he felt that way has been debated for many years. Some claim it was because Wagner was a nonsmoker and didn't want to set a bad example for children. According to the Baseball Hall of Fame, however, Wagner was a smoker but didn't want children to have to buy tobacco products to get his card. Whatever the reason, he ordered the American Tobacco Company to remove his picture from its cards.

Because few Honus Wagner cards were produced, the card became the most valuable baseball card of all time. Only fifty to sixty of the cards exist today. A 1909 Honus Wagner card sold for $2.35 million in 2007!

Before present-day regulations were adopted, tobacco companies advertised their product by sponsoring sporting events and putting their name on baseball cards, like this one.

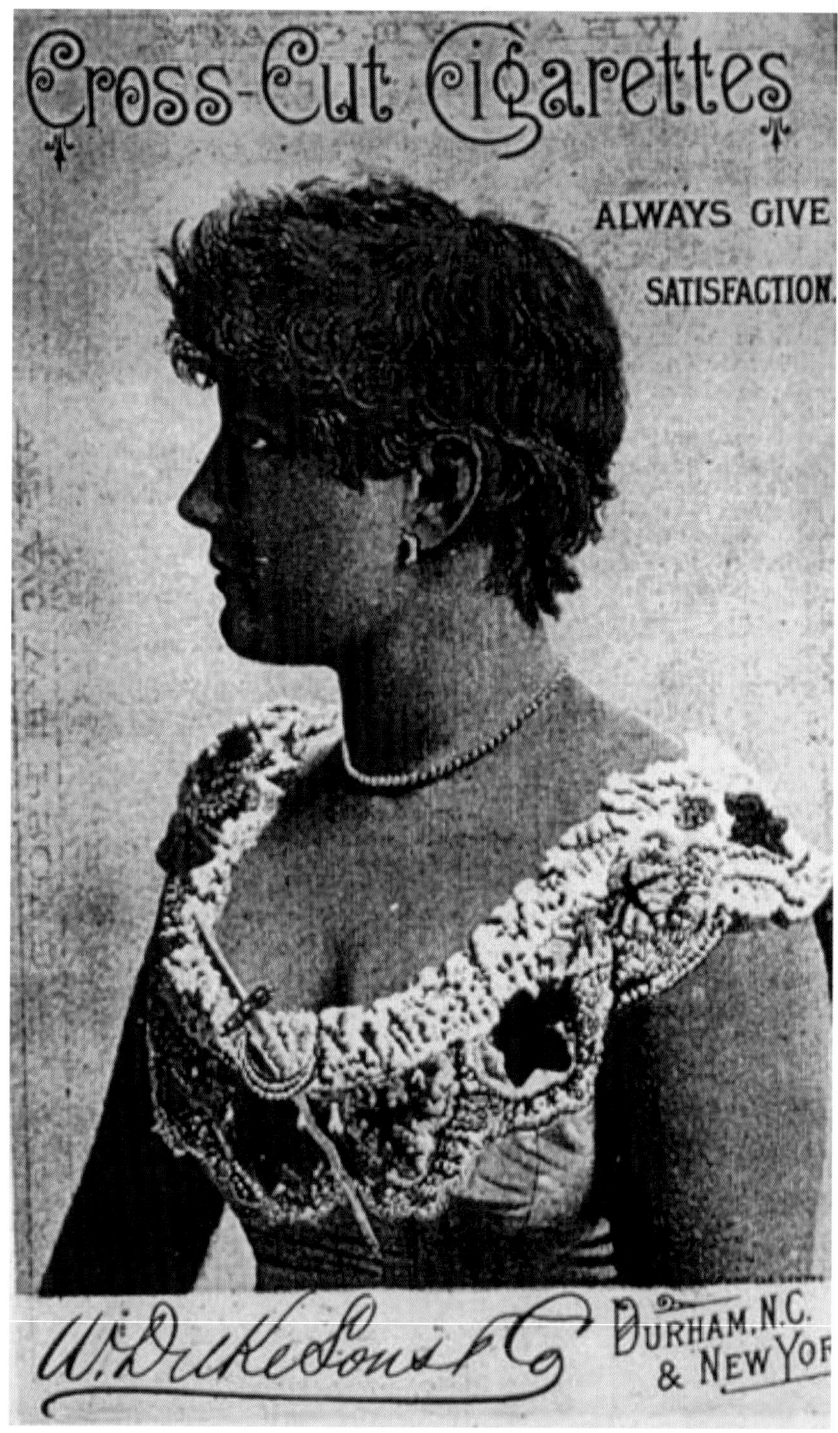

Cross Cuts was the first brand that was heavily advertised. Since Duke, cigarette brands have competed hard to gain customers that are loyal to their brands.

purchased a "dollar's worth of cigarettes" and didn't ask for a brand name. Duke wanted a name or a symbol that made his brand stand out. Cross Cuts is the name that was chosen.

To publicize his brand's name, Duke sponsored sports teams such as the Cross Cuts polo team and the Cross Cuts roller-skating team. These teams played in front of as many as 12,000 fans in their Cross Cuts jerseys. The next time fans bought cigarettes, the name Cross Cuts was fresh in their minds.

Duke and other cigarette manufacturers also began using cigarette packaging to their advantage. Not only was the company name and brand name displayed prominently on the package, but a free bonus was often placed inside each pack. Originally a piece of cardboard was stuck in the package to prevent the cigarettes from getting bent. Cigarette manufacturers decided to print different images on the cardboard as trading cards to add value to the pack. Each pack contained one card from a set. This enticed the smoker to buy several packages of the same brand to get the complete set of cards. Manufacturers produced sets with different themes—pictures of scantily clad women, stars of the stage, U.S. politicians, famous athletes, exotic animals, national monuments, flags of the world, and even British royalty.

Children loved to collect the cards. They begged their fathers to smoke more of a particular brand of cigarettes so they would get additional cards for their collections. And they often traded cards with their friends to get an entire set. Cigarette cards helped sell more cigarettes.

But the biggest reasons for Buck Duke's success were his aggressive advertising strategies and Bonsack's machines. In 1889 alone, W. Duke, Sons & Company spent $800,000—as much as 20 percent of the company's

This Camel cigarette pack shows an early version of the classic brand image.

profits—on advertising. This was more than any other cigarette company spent on advertising, and it worked. Whenever Duke ran a new advertising campaign, the company's cigarette sales jumped. Duke's competitors could only dream of making as much money as Duke did.

Give Me More!

Buck Duke was not satisfied with being number one. He wanted more; he wanted all the cigarette business in the

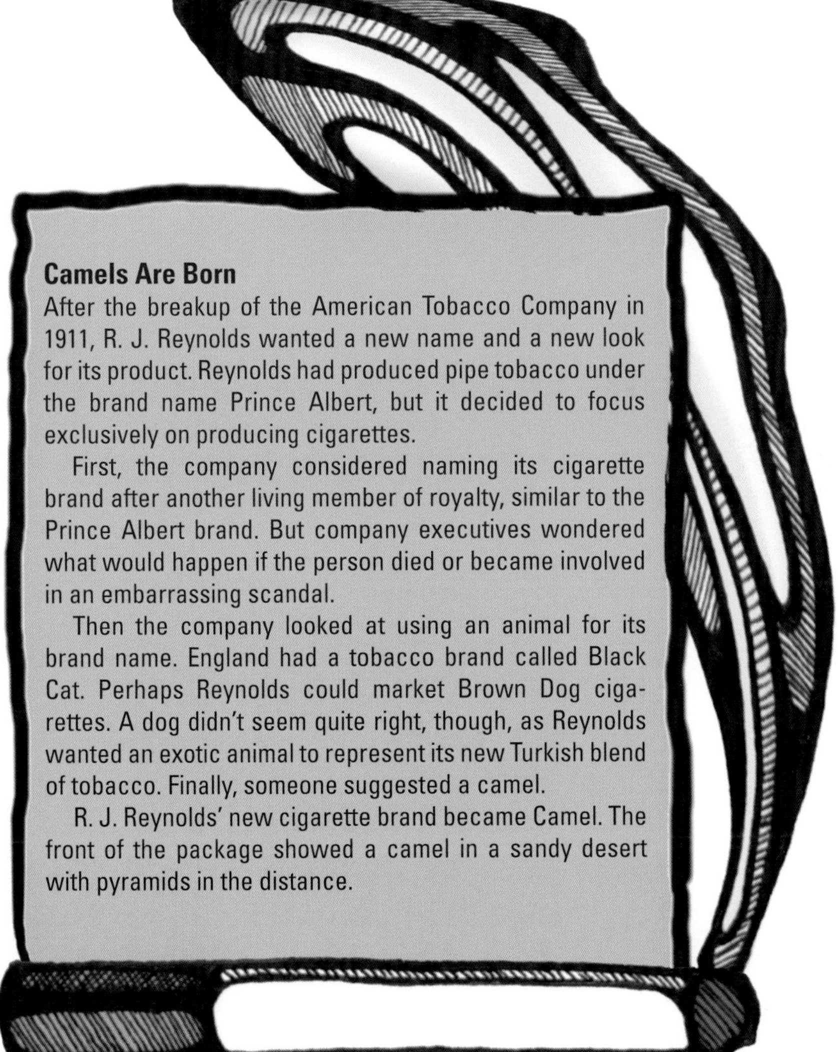

Camels Are Born

After the breakup of the American Tobacco Company in 1911, R. J. Reynolds wanted a new name and a new look for its product. Reynolds had produced pipe tobacco under the brand name Prince Albert, but it decided to focus exclusively on producing cigarettes.

First, the company considered naming its cigarette brand after another living member of royalty, similar to the Prince Albert brand. But company executives wondered what would happen if the person died or became involved in an embarrassing scandal.

Then the company looked at using an animal for its brand name. England had a tobacco brand called Black Cat. Perhaps Reynolds could market Brown Dog cigarettes. A dog didn't seem quite right, though, as Reynolds wanted an exotic animal to represent its new Turkish blend of tobacco. Finally, someone suggested a camel.

R. J. Reynolds' new cigarette brand became Camel. The front of the package showed a camel in a sandy desert with pyramids in the distance.

United States. With the money he made from selling so many cigarettes, he began buying out smaller, nonautomated cigarette manufacturers. Duke was the leader of the pack in the cigarette market, and no one could catch up.

In April 1889, Duke threatened to raise his advertising budget even more for the coming year. His competitors were upset because they knew they couldn't keep up with him. They had to do something before Duke owned their companies, too.

The four biggest companies met with Duke and reached a compromise. They decided to merge the five companies under the American Tobacco Company name. The president would be thirty-three-year-old Buck Duke.

The American Tobacco Company was able to purchase tobacco from growers at a lower price. The company also

President Harrison worried about the effects of monopolies on the economy; he worked to develop the Sherman Antitrust Act, which helped maintain competition.

set up a system to distribute tobacco products and combined its factories to make production more efficient. The American Tobacco Company became practically the only supplier of cigarettes in the United States. It basically had a *monopoly* on the production and distribution of cigarettes in the country.

The American Tobacco Company saturated the country with cigarettes, and soon sales leveled off. The company needed new smokers to buy the mountains of cigarettes it produced every day. It looked to England as a possible new market.

Duke went to England in September 1901 and began buying small tobacco companies there. The other British tobacco companies were furious and decided to beat Duke at his own game. The major British cigarette companies joined together to form the Imperial Tobacco Company. They offered to buy out the remaining independent American tobacco producers and put them under the Imperial Tobacco Company brand. They also bought up American retailers, which shut out American Tobacco Company brands from selling in those stores. The battle was fierce, but soon both sides called a truce.

The Imperial Tobacco Company and the American Tobacco Company agreed to a compromise in September 1902, limiting them to owning companies and selling tobacco products on their own soil. In addition, they formed a third, jointly owned company, the British American Tobacco Company. This company's mission was to sell tobacco outside England and the United States.

Too Big for Their Britches

In 1890 Congress had passed the Sherman Antitrust Act to help maintain competition in business. President Benjamin Harrison wanted to prevent monopolies or trusts

Buck Duke, the first president of the American Tobacco Company.

from controlling American businesses, such as oil and railroad companies. The American Tobacco Company claimed to be a *holding company*, not a monopoly, so it managed to get around this law for a time.

President Theodore Roosevelt and the Justice Department saw through the charade, however. On July 19, 1907, an antitrust (anti-monopoly) petition was filed against the American Tobacco Company, claiming it was monopolizing the cigarette industry. Duke and representatives from the American Tobacco Company testified before a grand jury that consumers benefited from their companies' merger. They said tobacco products were cheaper and better than before, and there were almost 100 brands for consumers to choose from.

On May 29, 1911, the U.S. Supreme Court rendered its decision: the American Tobacco Company was indeed a monopoly, and it had to be split into sixteen pieces. Four major companies emerged: Lorillard, Liggett & Myers, R. J. Reynolds, and a reorganized American Tobacco Company. The cigarette monopoly was also forced to sell off most of its holdings in the British American Tobacco Company. The remaining companies went in many different directions. Some decided to produce chewing or pipe tobacco, but most of the companies stayed with cigarettes.

Advertising and automated machines increased both production and sales of cigarettes, but war was also good for tobacco companies. Beginning with the Civil War and continuing through both world wars, combat increased both the number of people using cigarettes and the number of cigarettes they smoked.

CHAPTER 6

Words to Know

Allied forces: During World War II, an alliance of military forces whose most important members were Great Britain, the United States, and the Soviet Union.

subsidies: Grants from a government to support an organization.

Smoking During the World Wars

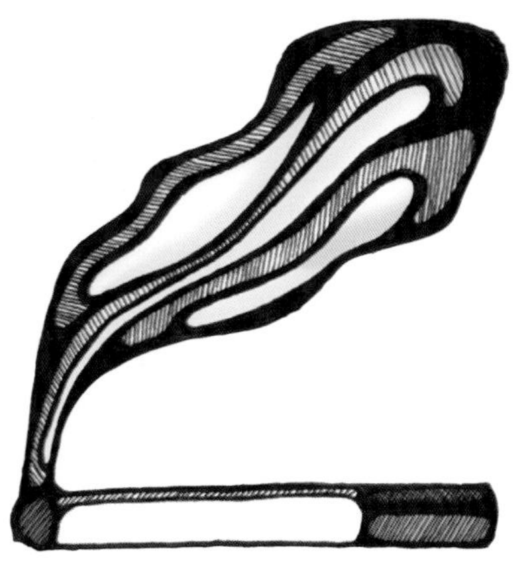

Cigarette smoking continued to gain popularity at the turn of the twentieth century. Increasing numbers of people found cigarettes easy to use, inexpensive, and portable. People didn't need anything fancy to smoke cigarettes, just a match and their smokes.

World War I had been going on in Europe for almost three years when the United States officially entered the fight on April 6, 1917. Four million American men would eventually serve in the army during the conflict. Many of the "doughboys," as the American troops were called, had been smokers before they landed in France. Most of those who hadn't previously smoked took up the habit during their time in the

For soldiers in WWI, smoking became a reminder of their homes and loved ones, as well as a way to escape the realities of war.

trenches. Men smoked as an escape from the realities of war and as an act of friendship between soldiers of all ranks. Wounded soldiers were given cigarettes to ease their pain and to remind them of home.

In Europe, American soldiers did not have ready access to cigarettes, as they did at home. In an effort to support the troops' tobacco habit, several organizations across the United States sponsored tobacco funds. They collected cigarettes, pipe tobacco, and money to buy

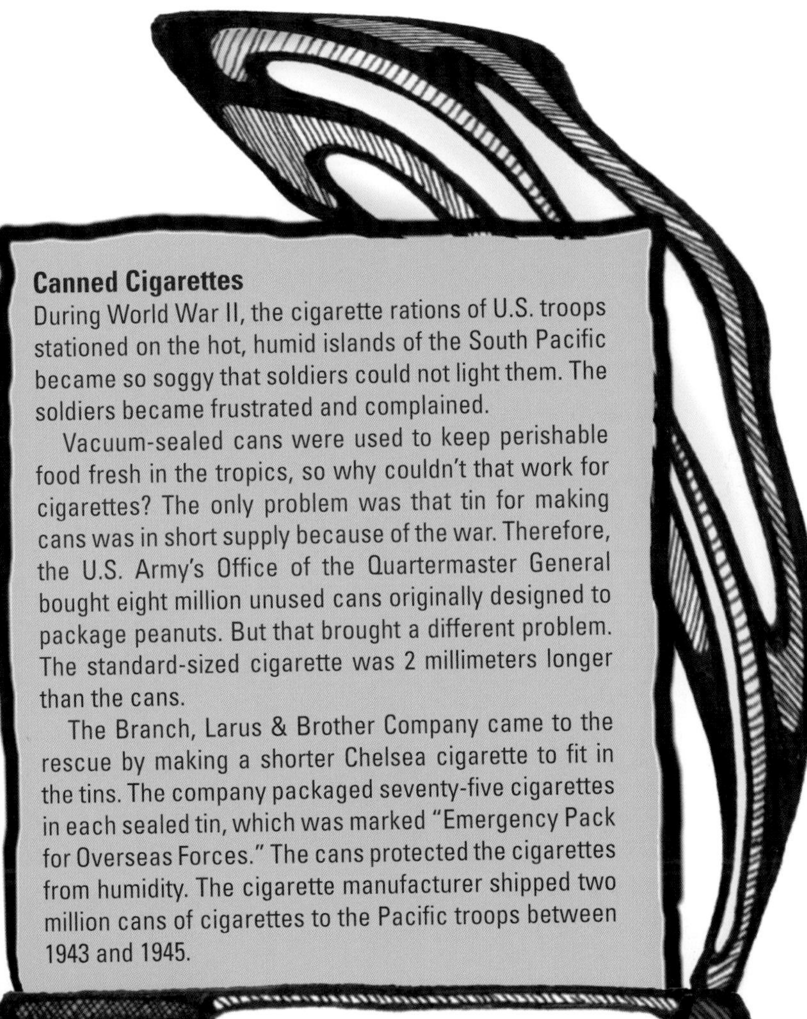

Canned Cigarettes

During World War II, the cigarette rations of U.S. troops stationed on the hot, humid islands of the South Pacific became so soggy that soldiers could not light them. The soldiers became frustrated and complained.

Vacuum-sealed cans were used to keep perishable food fresh in the tropics, so why couldn't that work for cigarettes? The only problem was that tin for making cans was in short supply because of the war. Therefore, the U.S. Army's Office of the Quartermaster General bought eight million unused cans originally designed to package peanuts. But that brought a different problem. The standard-sized cigarette was 2 millimeters longer than the cans.

The Branch, Larus & Brother Company came to the rescue by making a shorter Chelsea cigarette to fit in the tins. The company packaged seventy-five cigarettes in each sealed tin, which was marked "Emergency Pack for Overseas Forces." The cans protected the cigarettes from humidity. The cigarette manufacturer shipped two million cans of cigarettes to the Pacific troops between 1943 and 1945.

tobacco to ship to the troops. Groups included the North American Tobacco Fund, which began in 1917, and the Army Girl's Transport Tobacco Fund, begun in 1918. These groups placed newspaper ads asking for donations and put drop boxes in theaters. Children collected donations in their neighborhoods. Soon these organizations were shipping tobacco kits every day.

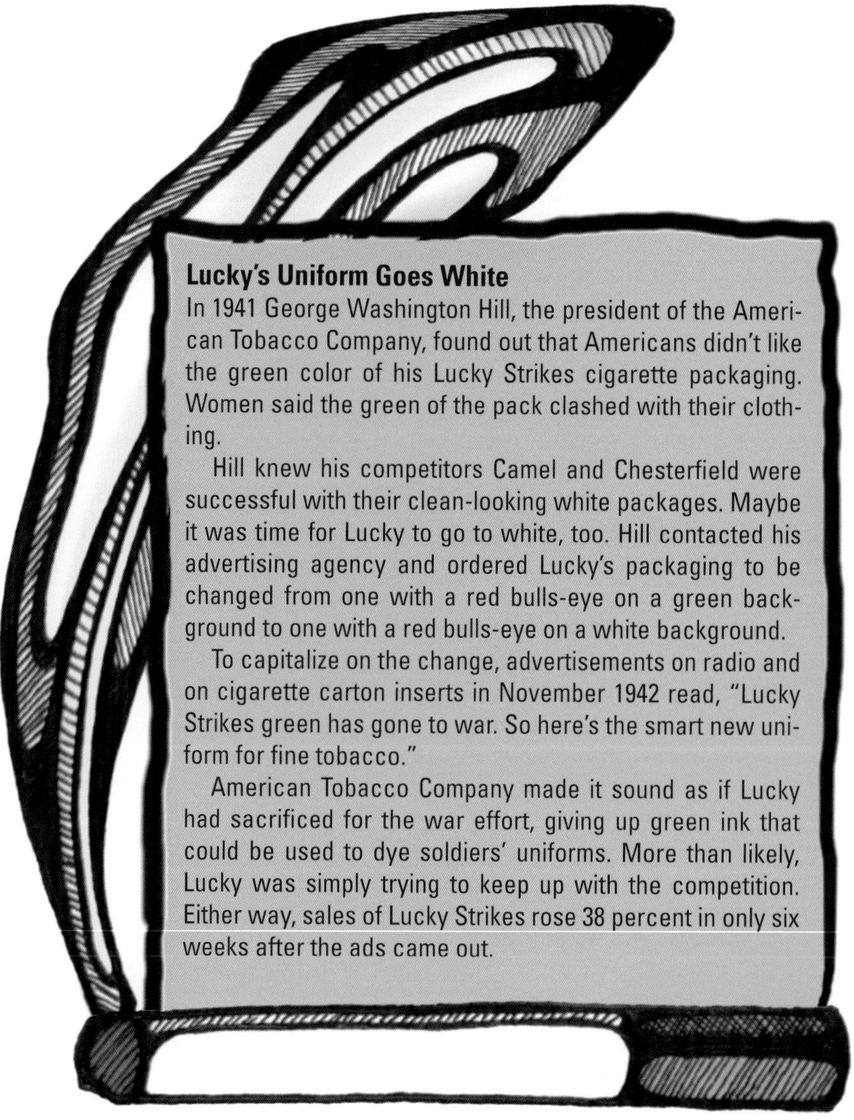

Lucky's Uniform Goes White

In 1941 George Washington Hill, the president of the American Tobacco Company, found out that Americans didn't like the green color of his Lucky Strikes cigarette packaging. Women said the green of the pack clashed with their clothing.

Hill knew his competitors Camel and Chesterfield were successful with their clean-looking white packages. Maybe it was time for Lucky to go to white, too. Hill contacted his advertising agency and ordered Lucky's packaging to be changed from one with a red bulls-eye on a green background to one with a red bulls-eye on a white background.

To capitalize on the change, advertisements on radio and on cigarette carton inserts in November 1942 read, "Lucky Strikes green has gone to war. So here's the smart new uniform for fine tobacco."

American Tobacco Company made it sound as if Lucky had sacrificed for the war effort, giving up green ink that could be used to dye soldiers' uniforms. More than likely, Lucky was simply trying to keep up with the competition. Either way, sales of Lucky Strikes rose 38 percent in only six weeks after the ads came out.

Tobacco was seen as necessity for soldiers at war.

In May 1918, the U.S. War Department stepped in, making certain tobacco was packed with the soldiers' food rations. Tobacco was seen as an essential item rather than a luxury. The War Department purchased cigarettes from U.S. manufacturers to send overseas. Most of the shipments contained R. J. Reynolds' Camel and America Tobacco Company's Lucky Strike brands. These two companies ran advertising campaigns in American magazines and newspapers, drawing attention to their support of the troops. The ads appealed to Americans' patriotism. And, along with the tobacco shipments sent overseas, they helped build brand loyalty.

Changes on the Home Front

The guns of World War I finally fell silent on November 11, 1918. Millions of American soldiers returned from the war as confirmed smokers.

While they had been fighting in Europe, important changes had taken place on the home front. Women had joined the workforce in record numbers, filling jobs vacated by soldiers. And whereas smoking had previously been considered unladylike, and relatively few

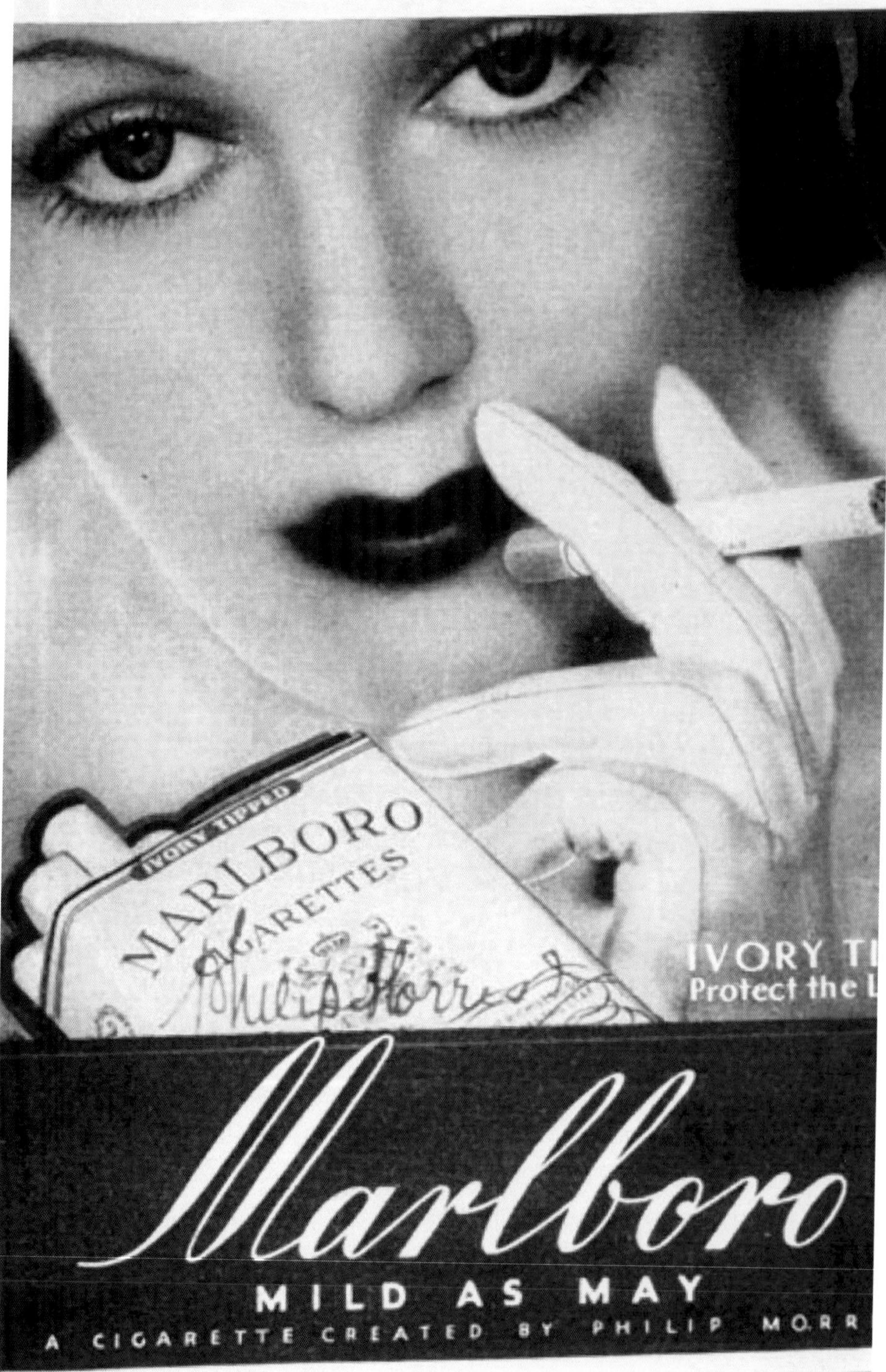

Marlboro cigarettes were initially marketed specifically for women, as seen in this early ad.

women had smoked in public, during the war many American women openly took up the habit.

There was growing sentiment for more equality between the sexes, and that sentiment found expression in the Nineteenth Amendment to the Constitution. The amendment, which was ratified on August 18, 1920, gave American women the right to vote.

Cigarette manufacturers raced to capitalize on women's newfound sense of equality—and on growing smoking rates among women. Philip Morris decided to create a cigarette just for women. The company came up with a lighter blend of tobacco and added a greaseproof ivory tip to prevent women's lipstick from smearing. The new brand was named Marlboro. In 1924 Philip Morris used the advertising slogan "Marlboro is as mild as May" to entice women to smoke the brand. Many women did indeed start smoking Marlboro cigarettes.

Lucky Strike also competed for female smokers. It, however, appealed to women's desire to stay thin. In the mid-1920s Lucky Strikes were marketed with the slogan "Reach for a Lucky, instead of a sweet." Sales of the brand shot up.

Legislating Fun

In 1919 the Eighteenth Amendment to the Constitution was ratified. It prohibited the manufacture, sale, and transportation of alcohol within the United States. The era of Prohibition had begun.

Some people feared that smoking would be banned next, but that didn't happen. During the 1920s, smoking increased dramatically. According to the Centers for Disease Control and Prevention, in 1920 Americans consumed over 44 billion cigarettes; by 1928, the number was over 100 billion!

Cigarettes and the Great Depression

The 1920s was an era of prosperity and exuberance in the United States; the decade was

During the Great Depression, the government subsidized farmers' land to ensure that there was no over-production of tobacco and to maintain demand.

appropriately dubbed the Roaring Twenties. But the good times came to an abrupt end in October 1929, when the stock market crashed, ushering in a long period of economic hardship known as the Great Depression. Large numbers of Americans lost their jobs, their homes, and their savings.

Still, tobacco companies' sales remained steady. Then, as now, people addicted to nicotine found it difficult to give up cigarette smoking, no matter how little money they had. Some people fed their addiction by reusing cigarette butts they found on the street. Stores sold individual cigarettes, "loosies," for one cent each; an entire pack of twenty cigarettes could cost fifteen cents. This was a lot of money during the Great Depression. Many times people only smoked half of a cigarette and saved the rest to enjoy later. Some people bought loose tobacco and rolled their own cigarettes.

In 1933 President Franklin D. Roosevelt launched the New Deal, a multifaceted program designed to help the country recover from the Great Depression. As part of the New Deal, Roosevelt signed into law the Agricultural Adjustment Act (AAA). The AAA paid farmers to cut back their production of staples such as tobacco and other crops by 30 percent. This made those crops more valuable since there was less available. The government paid the farmers ***subsidies*** to leave a portion of their fields unplanted.

Tobacco on the Big Screen

During the depths of the Great Depression, when unemployment rose to about 25 percent and millions of Americans were impoverished, motion pictures provided a temporary escape from the grim realities of daily life. On the flickering screens of movie theaters, Americans saw beautiful movie stars who didn't have to worry about money. They had mansions, yachts, fur coats, and diamond rings. They were decidedly glamorous, and they smoked frequently on-screen.

Different types of movie characters were portrayed with certain tobacco products. Pipe smokers were deep thinkers, such as detectives. Cigars symbolized power, and they were often smoked by actors portraying businessmen or gangsters. Cigarette smokers were sexy characters such as secretaries.

Tobacco companies were quick to announce which movie stars smoked their products. Stars like Bette Davis, Marlene Dietrich, Greta Garbo, Humphrey Bogart, Fred Astaire, Groucho Marx, and Al Jolson smoked on-screen. Tobacco companies paid stars to smoke their brand of cigarettes. Once fans found out which brand their favorite star smoked, they smoked that brand too. This helped boost sales tremendously.

Smoke 'Em if You Got 'Em

By 1941, Americans were smoking more than 200 billion cigarettes per year. On December 7 of that year, the Japanese bombed U.S. military facilities at Pearl Harbor, Hawaii. The attack on Pearl Harbor thrust the United States into World War II.

Servicemen needed their smokes more than ever. American soldiers, sailors, and airmen were obsessed with having enough cigarettes; it is said that some worried more about running out of smokes than about running out of ammunition. The government tried to make sure servicemen had enough of both. All branches of the armed forces provided cigarettes as part of their daily combat rations. In fact, U.S. servicemen were given five to seven packs of cigarettes per week. The saying "Smoke 'em if you got 'em" was popular between squad leaders and their troops. Officers often gave their men additional cigarettes before they went into battle to help calm the men's trembling hands, increase their efficiency, and distract them from upcoming dangers.

Other countries' smoking soldiers weren't so fortunate. Troops from Great Britain were given seven cigarettes per day. German troops received six cigarettes per

By WWII, soldiers were obsessed with their tobacco; cigarettes were considered almost as important as ammunition!

President Roosevelt was famous for using a cigarette holder to smoke.

day, even though their leader, Adolf Hitler, was very much against smoking. Hitler filled peoples' heads with antismoking slogans, banned smoking in public places, raised taxes on cigarettes, and was very opposed to women smoking.

Off the Battlefield

At home in America, civilians didn't have the ready access to cigarettes the men serving overseas did. There were constant shortages of cigarettes in cities like Philadelphia, Detroit, Chicago, and Atlanta. When word got out that a store was getting a cigarette shipment, lines quickly formed outside and snaked down the street. Some people camped out for days to buy cigarettes, as people do today for tickets to a big concert or sporting event. Sometimes scalpers at the front of the line bought several cartons of cigarettes and resold them to those at the end of the line when the store's shipment ran out. Scalpers worked under the law of supply and demand, charging up to thirty times the regular price. People were desperate for their cigarettes and paid outrageous prices for them.

The leaders of the *Allied forces* became well known for their preferences in smoking products and paraphernalia. President Franklin D. Roosevelt used a cigarette holder to smoke cigarettes. Winston Churchill of Great Britain smoked cigars. Joseph Stalin of the Soviet Union preferred a pipe.

Smoking was part of the war effort itself. During this era, tobacco helped everyone from soldiers to farmers to working women do their jobs better. But society's attitude toward tobacco wouldn't stay favorable.

CHAPTER 7

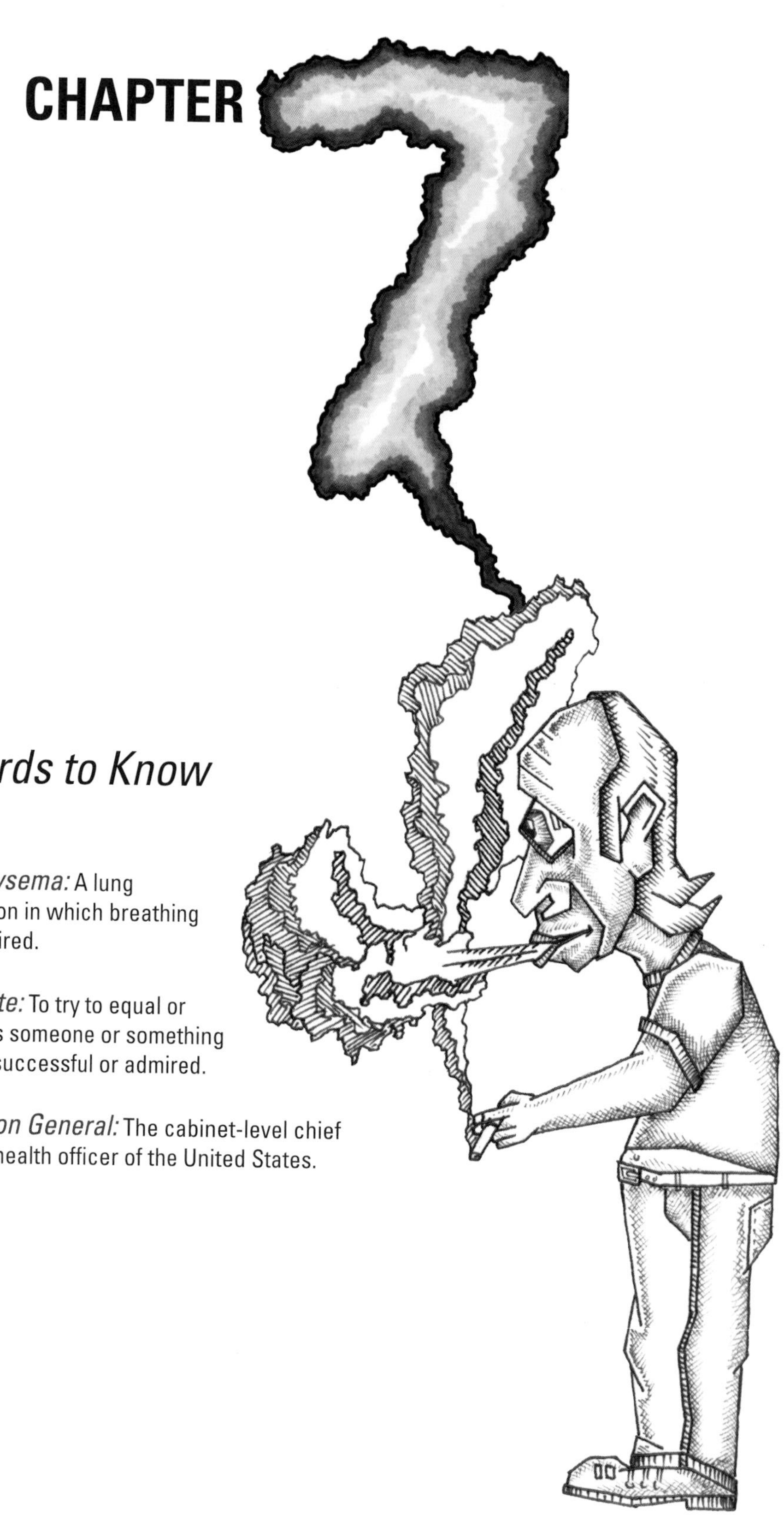

Words to Know

emphysema: A lung condition in which breathing is impaired.

emulate: To try to equal or surpass someone or something that is successful or admired.

Surgeon General: The cabinet-level chief public-health officer of the United States.

The Government Fights Back

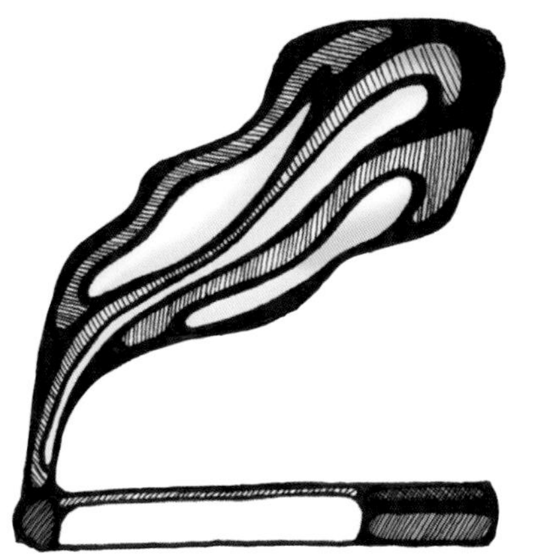

In 1945, with the conclusion of World War II, cigarette manufacturers had more customers than at any other time in their history. As was the case during previous conflicts, many servicemen had taken up smoking during the war, and most continued the habit once they returned to civilian life.

The postwar years were a time of great prosperity in the United States. Middle-class families saved and had enough money to live comfortably. People were able to afford luxuries the Great Depression generation had only dreamed about. These included new homes, cars, and plenty of cigarettes. Smoking soon became a fixture in American society, with about one-half of men and one-third of women smoking.

And a new generation would take up smoking enthusiastically during the 1950s. That decade saw the birth of rock and roll. Teens of the 1950s idolized and sought to *emulate* their favorite stars. Many of these early rock stars—such as Elvis Presley, Buddy Holly, Chuck Berry, and Jerry Lee Lewis—smoked.

Movies of the time were also filled with smokers popular with young Americans. Actors like James Dean smoked both on and off the screen. Teens who idolized Dean began dressing and smoking like him.

Cigarettes on the Small Screen

Another item that became familiar during the prosperous postwar years was the television set. Television brought entertainment and advertisers right into peoples' living rooms. Tobacco manufacturers saw this as an ideal way to speak directly to the consumer.

In 1950 Lucky Strike became the first cigarette brand to sponsor a TV show. The teen-oriented music series called *Your Hit Parade* was popular and ran for seven years. Lucky's advertisements ran during every commercial break.

Other cigarette manufacturers soon followed suit. In 1951 Philip Morris sponsored the television show *I Love Lucy.* This sitcom featured a red-headed smoker, Lucy Ricardo, who got into hilarious situations in every show. *I Love Lucy* was the most popular comedy of all time. This meant that a huge audience was viewing the Philip Morris cigarette commercials.

News programs were even clouded in a haze of smoke. Newsman John Cameron Swayze kept a pack of Camel cigarettes next to a smoldering cigarette in an ashtray on his desk. Not surprisingly, his program, *Camel News Caravan*, was sponsored by the cigarette company. The program refused to air any stories on the harmful effects of tobacco, and no airtime was given to people who were smoking unless they smoked Camel cigarettes. Still, nothing could stop the coming flood of antismoking news stories.

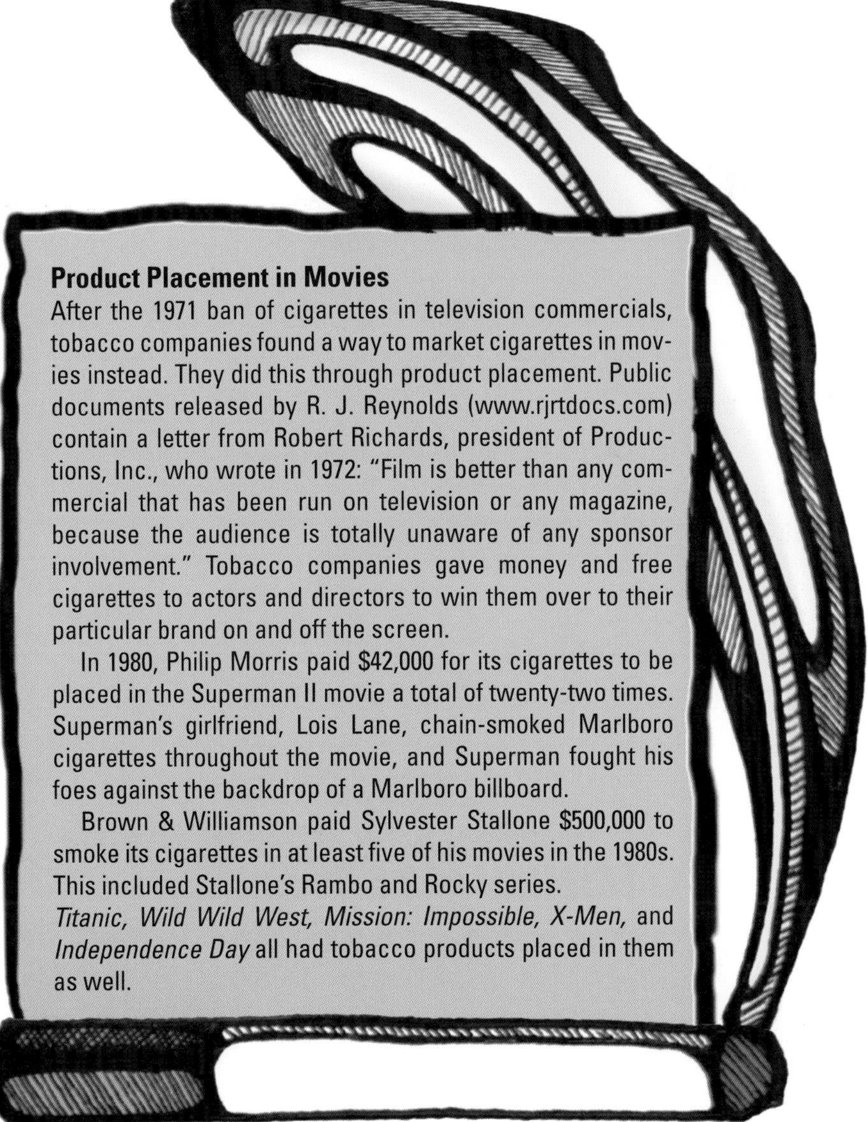

Product Placement in Movies

After the 1971 ban of cigarettes in television commercials, tobacco companies found a way to market cigarettes in movies instead. They did this through product placement. Public documents released by R. J. Reynolds (www.rjrtdocs.com) contain a letter from Robert Richards, president of Productions, Inc., who wrote in 1972: "Film is better than any commercial that has been run on television or any magazine, because the audience is totally unaware of any sponsor involvement." Tobacco companies gave money and free cigarettes to actors and directors to win them over to their particular brand on and off the screen.

In 1980, Philip Morris paid $42,000 for its cigarettes to be placed in the Superman II movie a total of twenty-two times. Superman's girlfriend, Lois Lane, chain-smoked Marlboro cigarettes throughout the movie, and Superman fought his foes against the backdrop of a Marlboro billboard.

Brown & Williamson paid Sylvester Stallone $500,000 to smoke its cigarettes in at least five of his movies in the 1980s. This included Stallone's Rambo and Rocky series.

Titanic, Wild Wild West, Mission: Impossible, X-Men, and *Independence Day* all had tobacco products placed in them as well.

Celebrities like Lucille Ball and Desi Arnaz advertised cigarettes, making them more appealing to many young Americans.

Masking the Problem

In 1952 the *Journal of the American Medical Association* published the results of research done by the American Cancer Society. The research found a link between smoking and lung cancer. Though average citizens might not have read the original article, when the research results were published in periodicals such as *Reader's Digest*, people began to pay attention. Between 1953 and 1954, consumption of cigarettes dropped 9 percent.

Cigarette manufacturers knew they had to respond or face a sales freefall. On January 4, 1954, cigarette manu-

Viceroy added cork filters to their cigarettes, claiming that this made them cleaner and healthier.

facturers paid for a statement placed in 448 American newspapers. Titled "A Frank Statement to Cigarette Smokers," it claimed that findings linking smoking and lung cancer were not conclusive.

Tobacco companies tried to make their product appear healthier. They looked to Viceroy, which had added cork filters to cigarettes in 1932. This, it was claimed, prevented tobacco from sticking to smokers' teeth and helped filter out impurities. Other cigarette manufacturers decided to add filters to their cigarettes in the 1950s. Cotton, asbestos, activated charcoal, and cellulose acetate were all used for filters. Tobacco companies told smokers they could enjoy cigarettes while the filter disposed of harmful risks. Unfortunately, this wasn't true.

In 1955 Americans smoked an average of 1,400 cigarettes per year, but less than 18 percent of the cigarettes were filtered. By 1963 Americans smoked an average of 4,000 cigarettes per year, and about 50 percent were filtered. Americans were smoking more cigarettes, and many believed the filter protected them from harm.

Health Warnings

On January 11, 1964, the ***Surgeon General*** of the U.S. Public Health Service announced that there was a link between smoking and lung cancer. Then, on January 1, 1966, the Federal Cigarette Labeling and Advertising Act went into effect. Cigarette manufacturers were forced to put a warning label on every pack of cigarettes. The warning read: "Caution: Cigarette Smoking May Be Hazardous to Your Health." Amazingly, cigarette sales rose by over 7.8 billion in 1966. Apparently people didn't take the warning seriously.

In 1967 the Federal Communications Commission (FCC) ruled that the "fairness doctrine" applied to cigarette commercials. For every tobacco ad on TV, networks were required to provide equal time to air warnings about the hazards of cigarettes. In 1968 alone, the three major networks aired 1,300 free anti-tobacco messages.

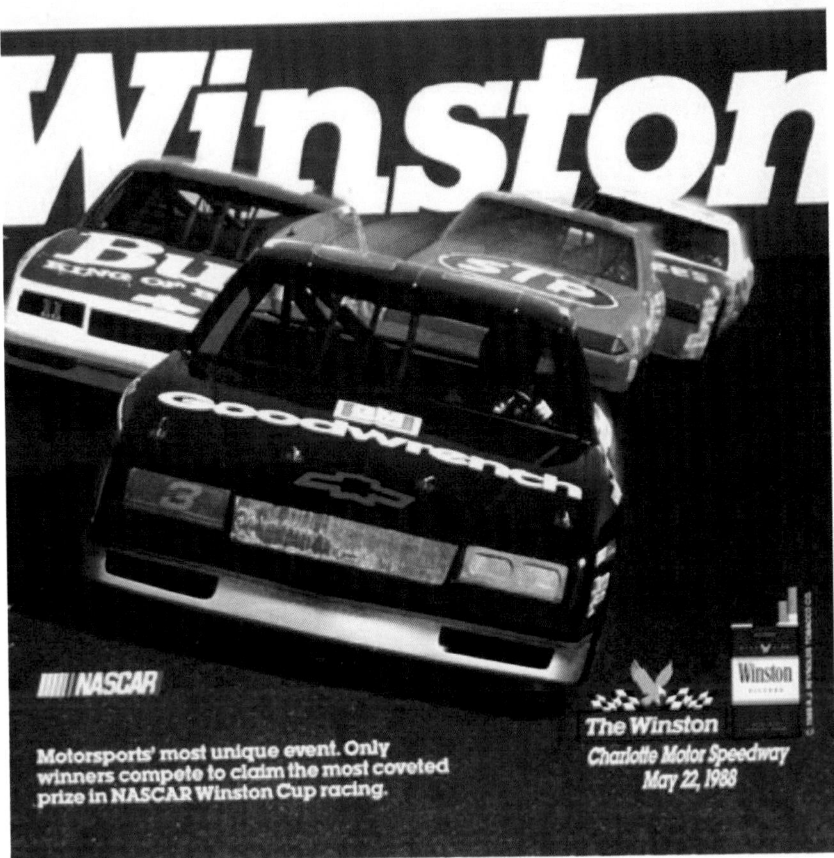

Cigarette companies sponsored various events, like this Winston drag race, in an attempt to advertise their product.

Before the MSA, tobacco companies were free to sponsor whatever events they wanted, like this concert.

Banning Cigarettes

In 1969 Congress passed the Public Health Cigarette Smoking Advertising Act. The act, signed into law in April 1970 by President Richard M. Nixon, banned cigarettes from being advertised on TV and radio. The act also required a stronger warning on cigarette packs. It read: "Warning: The Surgeon General Has Determined That Cigarette Smoking Is Dangerous To Your Health." This same warning had to appear on printed ads for

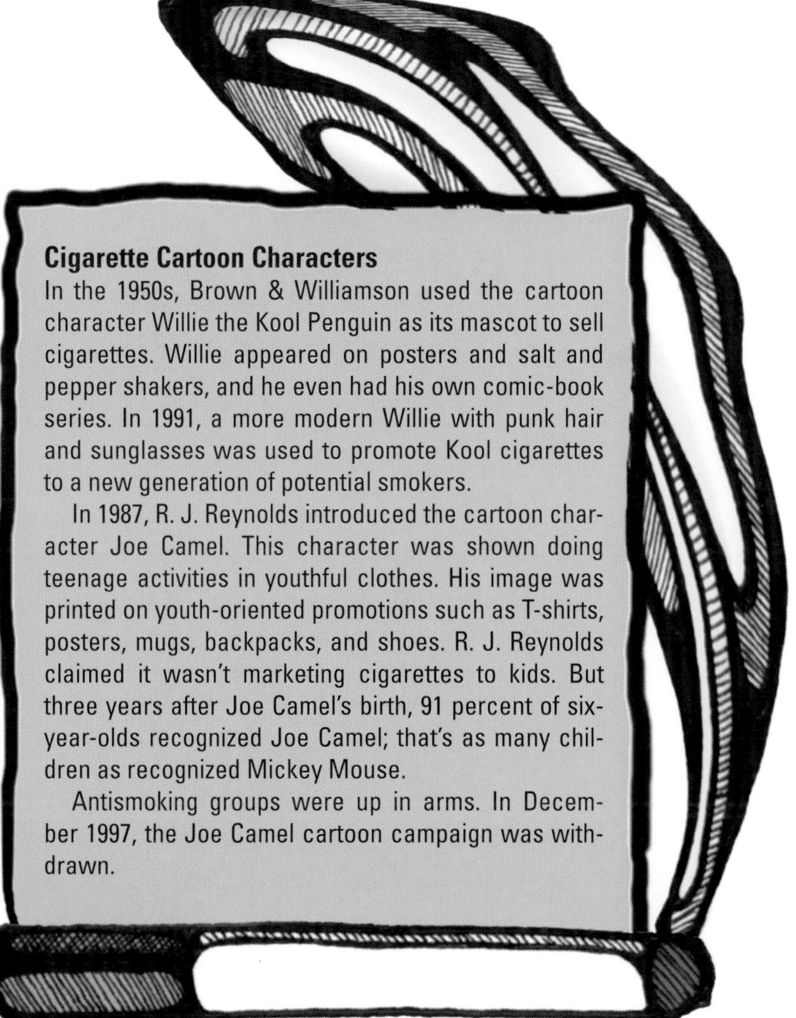

Cigarette Cartoon Characters

In the 1950s, Brown & Williamson used the cartoon character Willie the Kool Penguin as its mascot to sell cigarettes. Willie appeared on posters and salt and pepper shakers, and he even had his own comic-book series. In 1991, a more modern Willie with punk hair and sunglasses was used to promote Kool cigarettes to a new generation of potential smokers.

In 1987, R. J. Reynolds introduced the cartoon character Joe Camel. This character was shown doing teenage activities in youthful clothes. His image was printed on youth-oriented promotions such as T-shirts, posters, mugs, backpacks, and shoes. R. J. Reynolds claimed it wasn't marketing cigarettes to kids. But three years after Joe Camel's birth, 91 percent of six-year-olds recognized Joe Camel; that's as many children as recognized Mickey Mouse.

Antismoking groups were up in arms. In December 1997, the Joe Camel cartoon campaign was withdrawn.

cigarettes. The TV and radio ad ban went into effect on January 2, 1971.

With their ability to advertise on television and radio cut off, the tobacco companies had to look for other ways to promote their products. After 1971, they doubled their spending on magazine ads and quadrupled the dollars spent on newspaper ads.

Smart-thinking advertising agencies in the 1970s put cigarettes back on TV in a way that got around the

While the U.S. government has limited how tobacco is advertised, it still supports tobacco farmers through subsidies.

ban. Tobacco companies sponsored sporting and music events that were televised to millions of fans. Cigarette companies sponsored stock cars, so their logos were plastered all over the vehicles as they sped around the track. Cigarette logos were on banners around the racetrack as well. Tobacco companies sponsored sporting events such as the NASCAR Winston Cup races, the Virginia Slims women's tennis circuit, and the Marlboro Cup horse race. Tobacco companies also sponsored music events such as the Kool Jazz concert and the Marlboro Country Music Festival. Thus, clever marketing got around the law and put tobacco back on TV and in the public eye.

In 1973 the Civil Aeronautics Board required all U.S. airlines to establish smoking sections on planes. The only problem was that there was no wall to stop smoke from billowing from the smoking section to the nonsmoking section. In 1988 the U.S. Congress banned smoking on flights that were less than two hours long. And in 1990 smoking was banned on all domestic airline flights. A similar ban went into effect for trains in 1976 and buses on interstate trips in 1990.

Congress passed the Comprehensive Smoking Education Act in October 1984. It required cigarette companies to rotate warning messages on their packages every quarter. One warning listed the diseases smoking caused, one stated that quitting smoking would reduce health risks, one warned that smoking by pregnant women could cause fetal injury, and the other stated that cigarette smoke contains carbon monoxide.

The Master Settlement Agreement

As smoking's long-term health effects became known, many states found themselves burdened by the costs associated with treating illnesses such as lung cancer and *emphysema*. As their smoking populations became increasingly ill, the states' Medicaid spending rose as well. States looked to the tobacco companies for help. After all, many in government and in the health-care community believed it had been proved beyond a shadow of a doubt that tobacco companies had created the situation.

Many states began their attempts to recoup health-care costs by suing the tobacco companies. To avoid such litigation, the four major tobacco companies reached a compromise with forty-six state attorneys-general and representatives from six U.S. territories on November 23, 1998. (The other four states had already reached a settlement with the tobacco companies.) The Master Settlement Agreement (MSA) stated that the tobacco companies needed to pay the states $246 billion over the next twenty-five years as compensation for tobacco-related medical costs. It also prohibited cigarette advertising campaigns targeted at youth; cartoon promotions;

This cigarette rolling machine allows cigarettes to be produced quickly and cheaply, meaning that they can be easily distributed all over the world.

and ads on public transportation, on billboards, and in stadiums, arenas, and malls. Tobacco companies could no longer sponsor concerts and sporting events likely to have youth in attendance. Cigarette companies were to stop giving away samples and selling merchandise with tobacco logos. The MSA may have hurt the tobacco companies in various ways, forcing them to change the way they did business. But it also protected them from further lawsuits.

Beginning in 2002, another ban prohibited smoking inside government buildings in forty-five states. Secondhand smoke, the smoke breathed in by people not smoking, was a real concern. Many states and cities banned smoking in restaurants, workplaces, and even cabs. In 2007, in an action that reflected the growing concern about secondhand smoke's effects on children, some communities banned smoking around playground equipment in public parks. That same year, the New York City Council agreed to hear proposals to ban smoking in cars carrying children under the age of eighteen. Smokers had fewer and fewer places where they could enjoy their cigarettes.

What's Wrong with This Picture?

The relationship between government and tobacco is complex. In the days of federally imposed smoking bans, the U.S. government seemed to be contradicting itself by also supporting tobacco growers. The federal government has subsidized tobacco farmers since the 1933 Agricultural Adjustment Act went into effect. Before each growing season, the United States Department of Agriculture (USDA) established a minimum price for tobacco. Growers were each allotted a certain amount, or quota, of leaf they could bring to market. After the tobacco grew, it was sold at an auction house. If the leaf sold at a lower price than that set by the USDA, the Tobacco Cooperative Stabilization Corporation paid the grower the difference.

In 1986 the Omnibus Reconciliation Act gave manufacturers control over tobacco acreage allotments. A certain number of acres in the United States were allotted for growing tobacco. In 1995 tobacco earned $4,191 per acre, compared to $306 for cotton and $136 for wheat. Tobacco growers were paid the highest amount to any farmers in America. Tobacco had become a real cash cow for growers.

The tobacco industry has spent tens of millions of dollars to influence the opinions of politicians. For example, during the first six months of 2003 alone, the tobacco industry spent $10.6 million to lobby support in the U.S. Congress. Tobacco companies routinely contribute to the campaigns of senators and congressmen, and to the campaigns of presidential candidates. Clearly the industry hopes to get something in return.

With indisputable evidence of the harmful effects of cigarette smoking, government health agencies encouraged people to quit smoking. But the more people who smoked, the more money the government made on cigarette taxes. To discourage tobacco use could seriously affect the U.S. Treasury. The U.S. government found itself in a position similar to that of Napoleon III, emperor of France from 1852 to 1870. Napoleon said he would forbid the vice of smoking as soon as he could find a taxable virtue that brought in as much revenue as the tobacco tax. He couldn't.

For many years the tobacco industry and the public-health community have been engaged in a tug-of-war. Some observers believe that the reason the public-health community hasn't triumphed completely boils down to one factor: money. Tobacco farmers, cigarette manufacturers, and the U.S. government have grown as addicted to tobacco money as users are addicted to nicotine.

Reaching a World Market

Americans' smoking rate dropped 20 percent to 30 percent between 1990 and 2000. Tobacco consumption in the United States was so low that cigarette companies looked elsewhere for new smokers to buy their products, and they found them.

In the 1980s, American cigarette companies started selling aggressively to Third World countries. This has helped create a profitable market. Developing countries in Asia, for example, have seen smoking rates increase by 2 percent every year since 1982. As a result of this increase in foreign smokers, cigarette companies are making more money than ever before even though fewer Americans are smoking.

Tobacco began on a mountain in the Andes and has become a presence in every country of the world. It has influenced many aspects of American life. Tobacco has gone from being a cash crop that turned around the colonies, to a cash cow for the tobacco industry and tobacco growers through direct sales and subsidy programs.

Further Reading

Burns, Eric. *The Smoke of the Gods*. Philadelphia, Pa.: Temple University Press, 2007.

Gately, Iain. *Tobacco: A Cultural History of How an Exotic Plant Seduced Civilization*. New York: Grove Press, 2001.

Goodman, Jordan (ed.). *Tobacco in History and Culture: An Encyclopedia*. Farmington Hills, Mich.: Thomson Gale, 2005.

Hyde, Margaret, and John F. Setaro. *Smoking 101: An Overview for Teens*. Minneapolis, Minn.: Lerner, 2006.

Williams, Mary. *Smoking: At Issue*. Malvern, Australia: Tandem, 2003.

For More Information

Cigarette Advertising
www.wclynx.com/burntofferings/index.html

HYPERLINK "http://www.ibiblio.org/dukehome/family.html" Duke Family and Its Tobacco Empire
www.ibiblio.org/dukehome/family.html

FDA Authority over Tobacco
www.tobaccofreekids.org/reports/fda/chronology.shtml

Lewis and Clark Expedition- HYPERLINK "http://www.lewis-clark.org/content/content-article.asp?ArticleID=1358" Critical Tobacco Shortages
www.lewis-clark.org/content/content-article.asp?ArticleID=1359

The Tobacco Timeline
www.tobacco.org/History/Tobacco_History.html

Tobacco Under Attack—A Brief History of Tobacco
www.cnn.com/US/9705/tobacco/history/index.html

Walter Reed Brief History of Tobacco Use and Abuse
www.wramc.amedd.army.mil/Patients/diseases/wh/c7/Pages/s5.aspx

Bibliography

Ambrose, Stephen E. *Undaunted Courage*. New York: Simon & Schuster, 1996.

Clark, Robert. Supervisory Archivist, Franklin D. Roosevelt Presidential Library. Personal correspondence.

Courtwright, David T. *Forces of Habit: Drugs and the Making of the Modern World*. Cambridge, Mass.: Harvard University Press, 2001.

Derthick, Martha A. *Up in Smoke: From Legislation to Litigation in Tobacco Politics*. Washington, D.C.: CQ Press, 2005.

Devine, Tom. "The Tobacco Lords of Glasgow." *History Today* 40 (May 1990).

Forest, Angela. "Jamestown: Contradiction in Black and White." *Daily Press* (Newport News, Va.), February 18, 2007.

Graydon, Shari. *Made You Look: How Advertising Works and Why You Should Know*. Buffalo, N.Y.: Annick Press, 2003.

Haustein, Knut-Olaf. *Tobacco or Health? Physiological and Social Damages Caused by Tobacco Smoking*. Erfurt, Germany: Springer-Verlag Berlin Heidelberg, 2003.

Howland, Joyce. Science, Technology and Business Division, Library of Congress. Personal correspondence.

Hughes, Jason. *Learning to Smoke: Tobacco Use in the West*. Chicago: University of Chicago Press, 2003.

Jacobson, Peter D., and Jeffrey Wasserman. *Tobacco Control Laws: Implementation and Enforcement*. Santa Monica, Calif.: Rand, 2007.

Kills Small, Jerome. University of South Dakota American Indian Studies Instructor. Personal correspondence.

Kiple, Kenneth F. *The Cambridge World History of Human Disease*. Cambridge, UK: Cambridge University Press, 2003.

Kulifoff, Allan. *Tobacco and Slaves: The Development of Southern Cultures in the Chesapeake*, 1680–1800. Chapel Hill: University of North Carolina Press, 1986.

Mackay, Judith, Michael Eriksen, and Omar Shafey. *The Tobacco Atlas*. Atlanta, Ga.: American Cancer Society, 2006.

Moyer, David B. *The Tobacco Book: A Reference Guide of Facts, Figures, and Quotations About Tobacco*. Santa Fe, N.M.: Sunstone Press, 2005.

Ng, Crystal, and Bradley Dakake. *Tobacco at the Movies: Tobacco Use in PG-13 Films*. Boston: Massachusetts Public Interest Research Group Education Fund, 2002.

Petkofsky, Andrew. "Tobacco Seed Yields Clues About Jamestown." *Richmond Times-Dispatch*, January 11, 2007.

Proctor, Robert N. *The Nazi War on Cancer.* Princeton, N.J.: Princeton University Press, 1999.

Quintal, Margaret. University of South Dakota American Indian Studies Program Assistant. Personal correspondence.

Rabin, Robert L., and Stephen D. Sugarman. *Regulating Tobacco*. New York: Oxford University Press, 2001.

Remini, Robert V. *The Life of Andrew Jackson*. New York: Harper & Row Publishing, Inc., 1988.

Rogozinski, Jan. *Smokeless Tobacco in the Western World: 1550–1950*. New York: Praeger, 1990.

Snell, Clete. *Peddling Poison: The Tobacco Industry and Kids*. New York: Praeger, 2005.

St. John Erickson, Mark. "Jamestown Discovery: The Seed that Saved Virginia." *Daily Press* (Newport News, Va.), January 10, 2007.

Winter, Joseph C. (ed.). *Tobacco Use by Native North Americans: Sacred Smoke and Silent Killer*. Norman: University of Oklahoma Press, 2000.

Zobel, James. MacArthur Memorial Library & Archives of Norfolk, Virginia. Personal correspondence.

Index

Picture Credits

CIA World FactBook: p. 16

Dreamstime.com
Bobbiholmes, 57

Jupiter Images 12, 46–47

Library of Congress Prints and Photographs Division: pp. 15, 18, 24, 26, 42, 44, 51, 52, 54, 62, 65, 70, 82, 86

National Archives and Records Administration
58, 85

National Library of Medicine: pp. 28, 30, 32, 36

Northwestern University Library: pp. 20

Patrick Reynolds Collection, 72, 76

Tobaccodocuments.org
American Tobacco Co.: p. 79
Marlboro: p. 96
Philip Morris: p. 80, 92, 93
RJ Reynolds Tobacco Co: p. 68, 95
W. Duke Sons & Co: p. 66

U.S. Department of Agriculture
Hammond, Ken pp. 39, 98

To the best knowledge of the publisher, all other images are in the public domain. If any image has been inadvertently uncredited, please notify Harding House Publishing Service, Vestal, New York 13850, so that rectification can be made for future printings.

Author/Consultant Biographies

Author

Mary Meinking is a nonfiction children's author and a graphic designer. Her writing has appeared in many children's magazines. She lives with her family in northwest Iowa. They enjoy visiting historical sites while traveling around America.

The author dedicates this book to her parents, Norm and Nelda Meinking, who supported her artistic dreams and passed on their love of history and travel.

Consultant

Wade Berrettini, the consultant for *Smoking: The Dangerous Addiction*, received his MD from Jefferson Medical College and a PhD in Pharmacology from Thomas Jefferson University. For ten years, Dr. Berrettini served as a Fellow at the National Institutes of Health in Bethesda, Maryland, where he studied the genetics of behavioral disorders. Currently Dr. Berrettini is the Karl E. Rickels Professor of Psychiatry and Director, Center for Neurobiology and Behavior at the University of Pennsylvania in Philadelphia. He is also an attending physician at the Hospital of the University of Pennsylvania.

Dr. Berrettini is the author or co-author of more than 250 scientific articles as well as several books. He has conducted ground-breaking genetic research in nicotine addiction. He is the holder of two patents and the recipient of several awards, including recognition by Best Doctors in America 2003–2004, 2005–2006, and 2007–2008.